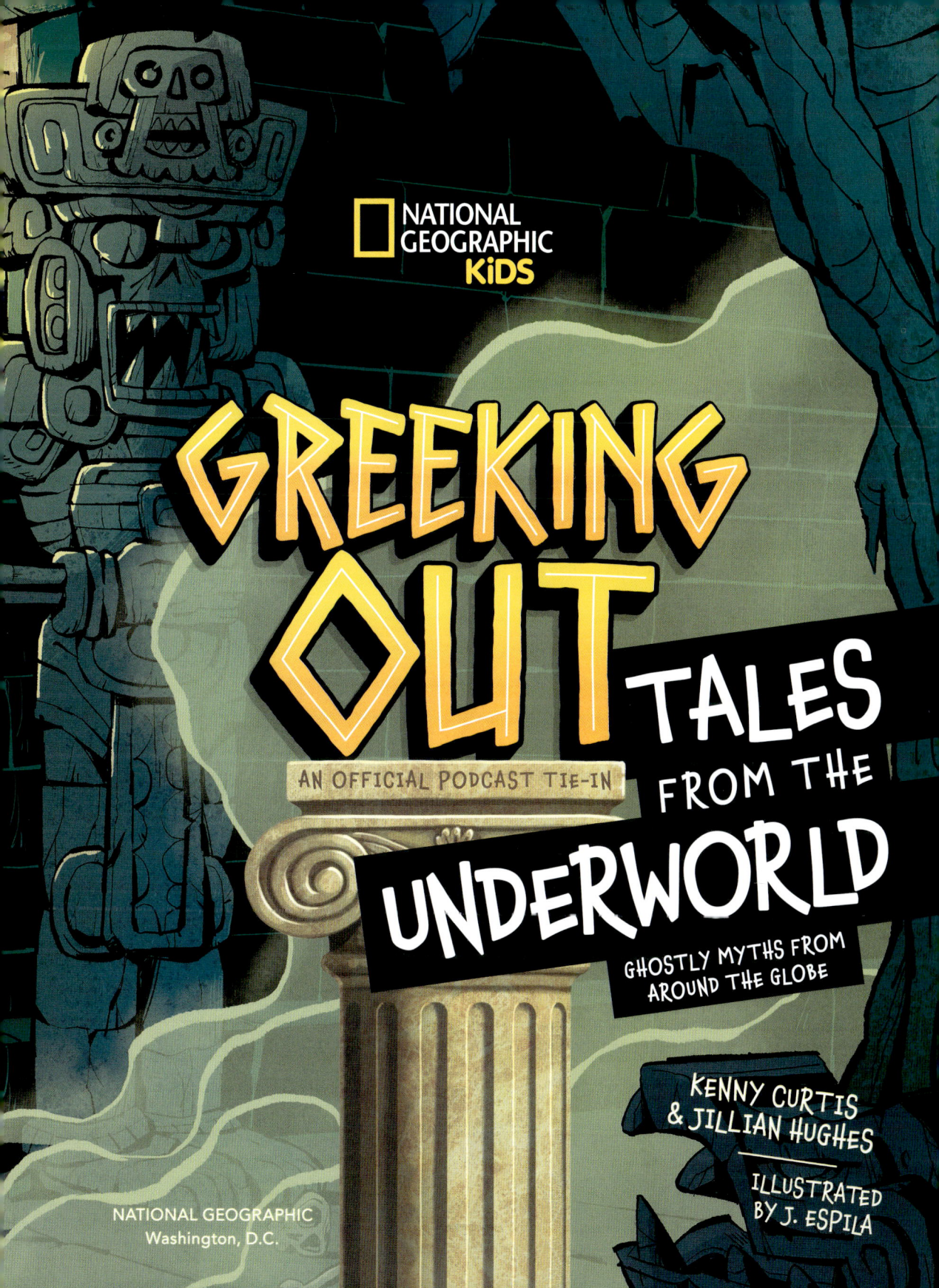

NATIONAL GEOGRAPHIC KiDS

GREEKING OUT

AN OFFICIAL PODCAST TIE-IN

TALES FROM THE UNDERWORLD

GHOSTLY MYTHS FROM AROUND THE GLOBE

KENNY CURTIS
& JILLIAN HUGHES

ILLUSTRATED
BY J. ESPILA

NATIONAL GEOGRAPHIC
Washington, D.C.

TABLE OF CONTENTS

HOLY HADES!

Since the beginning of time, human beings have wrestled with some really big questions: Why are we here? Why does time only move forward? And what do you call that little metal thing right below the eraser on a pencil?

But the biggest question has always been this: What happens after we die?

We know, we know. Death is not exactly a pleasant thing to talk about. Most of us tend to avoid the topic at parties. And yet ... it kind of seems like we humans can't stop thinking about it.

All over the world and all throughout history, different cultures have come up with thousands of stories about what happens after a person dies. Some are myths. Some are folktales. Some are scary movies with zombies that walk so slow you almost feel sorry for them. But each one paints a slightly different picture of the great beyond. There are literal underground Underworlds, heavenly palaces in the sky, and general mysterious spirit realms. But it's clear that people have been trying to crack this whole mystery-of-the-afterlife thing pretty much since forever, and ancient cultures told a lot of really incredible stories to help them think it through.

In our two previous books, we included a bunch of these stories from

Greek mythology.

Remember all those gods and heroes,

like Orpheus, Persephone, and Heracles, who journeyed into

the Underworld for one reason or another? In the pages that follow, we will tell you tales of even *more* Greek heroes who wound up encountering the Underworld, like Theseus, Odysseus, and Psyche.

But this time, we're taking things even further!

In these pages, we're going on an extended field trip to bring you a peek at the Underworld from *around the world*. Practically every ancient culture seems to have had a slightly different way of characterizing death and the Underworld, so in this book we're going to explore them all! Well, not really. We're going to explore a few of our favorites! With plenty of stops back in ancient Greece, we'll be traveling from Mesopotamia to Mexico, from Ireland to India, all in search of answers to those big life-and-death questions.

You'll see the Norse god Loki scheme to trap a rival in the Underworld, and the West African god Tano try to outrun Death himself. You'll learn how the Egyptian sun god Ra has to travel through the Underworld every night before he can move the sun through the sky every day. You'll encounter a surprising number of love stories and at least one room full of flying knives.

So consider this your invitation to a story-filled celebration of life in the afterlife. Let's get this party started!

Meet the Oracle of Wi-Fi

I AM THE ORACLE OF WI-FI. AS IN PREVIOUS BOOKS, I WILL APPEAR FROM TIME TO TIME TO OFFER FAST FACTS, ADD CLARIFICATIONS, AND THROW DOWN SOME GENERAL KNOWLEDGE. SO PLEASE KEEP YOUR EYE OUT FOR MY "EYE-CON" AND PILLAR TO GET SOME REAL ORACLE-STYLE WISDOM. ALSO, THE LITTLE METAL THING RIGHT BELOW THE ERASER ON A PENCIL IS CALLED THE FERRULE. NOW YOU KNOW.

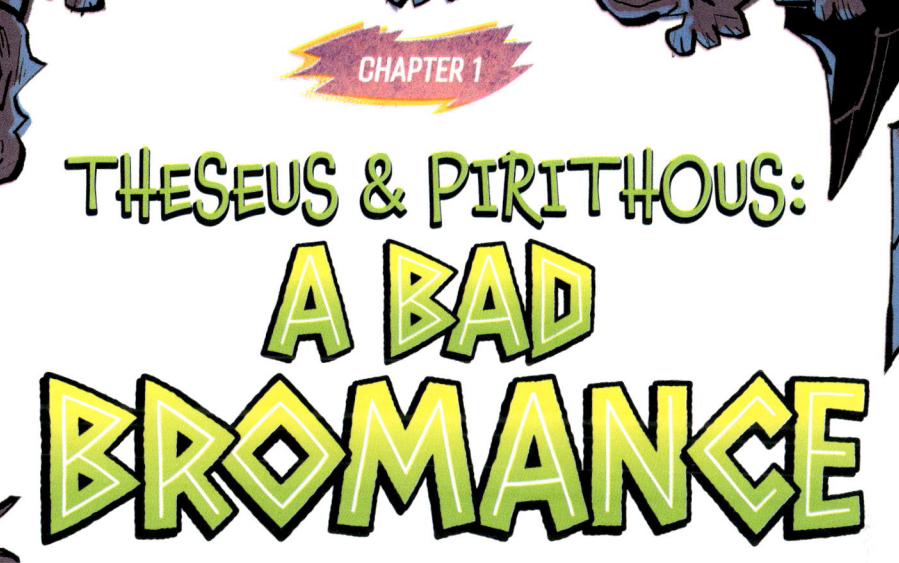

CHAPTER 1

THESEUS & PIRITHOUS:
A BAD BROMANCE

This tale features arrogant demigods, a Heracles cameo, a really sore butt, and some super-duper bad ideas.

T hings were going pretty well for Theseus. After defeating the monstrous Minotaur and becoming king of Athens, he was pretty much the golden boy of ancient Greece. (Because Poseidon may have been his dad, this wasn't particularly surprising.)

Theseus had caught the attention of almost everyone in Greece, including another famous demigod: Pirithous. Pirithous was the son of Zeus, and he was the king of the Lapiths in a region of ancient Greece called Thessaly. But he was still intrigued by Theseus. He had never met him, and he was interested in seeing just how talented the guy really was.

One day, Pirithous played a trick on Theseus. He stole all his cattle. Now if you've read any of these stories before (or listened to the *Greeking Out* podcast), you know how seriously the ancient Greeks took their cows. Theseus was *not* amused. When he realized that it was Pirithous who had stolen his precious cattle, he tracked the other king down and immediately challenged him to combat.

"What kind of king steals another man's cows? Have you no respect?!" Theseus bellowed.

The two demigods traded blows for a short time, but it wasn't long before Pirithous realized that he might be in over his head. Theseus was just as talented a swordsman as everyone had said. And while Pirithous wasn't too shabby himself, he decided to yield and apologize to Theseus.

"Look, my bad. I just wanted to meet you. You might not have heard, but you have quite a reputation!"

After that, the two became fast friends. Pirithous even invited Theseus to his wedding. (This turned out to be a good thing because some rowdy centaur wedding guests got way out of control, and Theseus had to help keep everyone in line.)

But life wasn't all victory laps for Theseus. He suffered some big losses as well. For example, when his wife Phaedra died, Theseus was understandably depressed. And that may have been what led to one of the worst decisions in all of Greek mythology.

As bad luck would have it, Pirithous had recently suffered a similar fate. His beautiful wife, Hippodamia, died, and he was devastated. He decided to visit Theseus, and after spending a few days moping around Athens, Pirithous and Theseus arrived at a (terrible) idea. They decided that they needed wives to make themselves happy. But because they didn't ever want to feel the sadness of losing a loved one again, they chose to pursue divine wives—specifically the daughters of Zeus—who were way less likely to die.

Now this idea was wrong for many reasons—most important is that women are not property to be claimed or stolen. People should, you know,

A DEMIGOD IS A PERSON WITH ONE MORTAL PARENT AND ONE DIVINE PARENT OR GRANDPARENT. IN GREEK MYTHOLOGY, MOST OF THESE DEMIGODS WERE CHILDREN OF ZEUS. SOME SAY HE HAD AROUND A HUNDRED CHILDREN!

want to get married. But to make matters worse, Theseus and Pirithous had their eyes on two particular brides, neither of whom was actually available.

Theseus had his heart set on young Helen of Sparta (soon to become Helen of Troy). So Theseus and Pirithous stole Helen away and took her to Theseus's kingdom, where he planned to hold her until he was ready to make her his queen.

This was *very* wrong, but, surprisingly, not the worst idea these guys came up with. Here was their worst idea: Pirithous wanted to kidnap the goddess Persephone and marry her. As you might know, Persephone was already married by this time. And not only was she already married, she was married to Hades, god of the Underworld. (Have we mentioned how incredibly bad this idea was?)

Theseus knew this was a bad idea and tried to talk his friend out of it. But Pirithous was stubborn and determined, and Theseus was honor bound to be his wingman.

The two kings made the long trip down into the Underworld and eventually found themselves on the banks of a black river. There was very little light, but they could just make out a small pier with a boat tethered to it. Standing on the dock by the boat was a tall man in a dark hood. He said nothing, but he gestured toward the boat with his hand, clearly inviting Pirithous and Theseus to come aboard.

"It seems we are expected," said Pirithous.

"Yeah ... I'm not so sure that's a good thing," Theseus replied.

The two kings pressed forward despite Theseus's misgivings. When the boat docked

IN GREEK MYTHOLOGY, CHARON WAS THE FERRYMAN OF THE UNDERWORLD. HE HAD A PRETTY SIMPLE JOB: HE WAS SUPPOSED TO CARRY THE SOULS OF THE RECENTLY DEPARTED ACROSS THE RIVER STYX, WHICH SEPARATES THE WORLDS OF THE LIVING AND THE DEAD.

on the other side of the river, Pirithous and Theseus weren't sure where to go. They hadn't thought this through very well. It's not like Pirithous could get the GPS coordinates of Persephone's location on his phone. They were going to have to search for her, and the search was going to take a while.

Turns out, the search took a *really* long while. Days, in fact! Finally, just when Pirithous and Theseus were ready to give up, Theseus heard the faint sound of a beautiful melody off in the distance.

"Did you hear that?" Theseus asked.

"Hear what?" Pirithous snapped. "I can't hear anything over the rumbling of my stomach. I'm starving and exhausted! And I still don't have a bride!"

But Theseus shushed his friend and listened harder. He could just make out some light music coming from a tunnel on the far left. He grabbed his torch and headed down the tunnel.

By the time they reached the end of the passage, the light had changed so much that the two demigods had to squint at the brightness coming from the room before them. They were in a dining hall with a banquet table prepared for a feast. In the far corner, a harp was playing by itself—which was a bit weird, but Theseus and Pirithous barely noticed. All their attention was focused on the table in front of them. Their mouths began to water at the sight of the amazing feast. It looked and smelled delicious.

"Greetings, kings," a voice boomed. "Welcome to my table. I am Hades, god of the Underworld, and you are my welcome guests. Please, sit."

Immediately, Pirithous and Theseus pulled out chairs and sat down, ready to dig in. In some part of their minds, they must have known this was yet another bad idea. They were here to kidnap the wife of Hades, and it definitely seemed like he'd been expecting them. But after days of wandering through dark tunnels, they were too exhausted and hungry to care.

They couldn't see Hades clearly. In the shadows, just past the far end of the table, they could make out the outline of a tall crowned man.

They also didn't seem to notice that their chairs had become a little more snug, as they were too focused on the feast before them.

"I hope you enjoy your stay in the Underworld," Hades continued. "I suspect it will be a longer visit than you originally planned."

With that, the shadow vanished. Pirithous and Theseus looked at one another, shrugged, and reached for the table ... which moved away, just out of reach. Or perhaps the table stayed still and their chairs moved back. It was hard to tell. But either way, Theseus and Pirithous were trapped. They were starving, and their mouths were watering. But no matter what they did, they could not reach the delicious feast that was quite literally inches away.

When the men tried to stand, they found that it was impossible. They couldn't get up from their chairs! Somehow they were bound by magic to the heavy stone seats. The two kings struggled and struggled, but it was no use. They could not leave the banquet, and they could not eat!

Historians believe that the first known chair was created in Egypt around 5,800 years ago when artisans added a backrest to a bench.

They yelled. They screamed. They even tried to knock each other out of their chairs, but nothing worked. Theseus and Pirithous were confused and scared. They began to suspect that maybe Hades had known about their plan from the beginning.

"He did this on purpose! We're stuck here forever!" Pirithous cried.

While we don't know exactly how long they were stuck, we do know that the demigods were trapped in the Underworld for a long time—years, even. And during these years, they never stopped being hungry, and they never got even a tiny crumb of food from the feast before them.

But eventually, there *was* a rescue! Well ... kind of. The mighty hero Heracles had been given the seemingly impossible task of "borrowing" Cerberus, the three-headed guard dog, from Hades. And while he was adventuring through the Underworld, Heracles stumbled upon two very beat-up looking kings trapped in some stone chairs.

"Heracles! HELP US! PLEASE!" they begged the famous hero.

But even the mighty Heracles had trouble with this one. He used all his godlike muscles and divine strength, but he could not pull the men free from their chairs. Every time he tried to lift Pirithous, the ground began to tremble

and the ceiling in the hall began to crack and crumble. The tremors got so bad that Heracles feared for all their lives. Making a quick decision, Heracles turned and pulled Theseus up with all of his might, finally freeing him from the chair—just in time to avoid being crushed by falling stone. Theseus was free, but Pirithous was trapped behind a wall of rocks and had to remain in the Underworld forever.

"No! Don't leave me!" he cried out.

"Sorry, buddy," Heracles said. "But this place *really* doesn't want you to leave. Trying to steal Hades' wife?! What were you thinking?"

When Theseus returned home to Athens, he discovered that he had lost something else. While he was trapped in the Underworld, Castor and Pollux, Helen of Sparta's brothers, had come to her rescue. She was now safe and sound back in Sparta, and Theseus was alone again—with nothing but a sore backside and a head full of regret.

IN ONE VERSION OF THE STORY, HERACLES WASN'T ACTUALLY ABLE TO FREE ALL OF THESEUS. HE LEFT THE MAN'S BUTTOCKS BEHIND, STILL ATTACHED TO THE CHAIR! FOR THIS REASON, THESEUS WAS SOMETIMES CALLED HYPOLISPOS, WHICH MEANS "WITH HIND PARTS RUBBED SMOOTH" (I SUSPECT PEOPLE DID NOT CALL HIM THAT TO HIS FACE).

In a lot of these myths, the term "hubris" comes up. Hubris is basically excessive pride and arrogance toward the gods, and it's something the ancient Greeks (and especially the Olympians) detested. Kidnapping Helen was a terrible thing to do, but trying to steal the wife of Hades was terrible *and* an insult to the gods. This is why Theseus was allowed to leave the Underworld, but Pirithous was not. Either way, it's important to think through your choices carefully, even when your friends are all in. It's good to have a pal who will have your back no matter what ... but it's also important to have friends who will help keep you from going too far off the path. Pro tip: If it involves the Underworld, it's too far off the path.

SOMETIMES SOMETHING SEEMS LIKE A GOOD IDEA, BUT LATER YOU DISCOVER IT WAS NOT. ON A RELATED NOTE: I HAVE RECENTLY DECIDED NOT TO MOVE FORWARD WITH MY PLAN TO BUILD AND SELL TREADMILLS FOR SNAKES.

ALL ABOUT HADES

He's the king of the dead, the lord of darkness, and the Underworld's God of the Year every year running. Ladies and gentlemen, we give you: *Hades!*

You're probably at least a little familiar with the Greek king of the Underworld. Hades shows up in a ton of stories and tales (more than we're able to share in this particular book). Here are some iconic moments and memories from Hades' long (and slightly scary) history.

DRAWING THE SHORT STRAW

Hades was one of the original Olympians, along with Zeus, Poseidon, Hera, Hestia, and Demeter. After Zeus rescued his siblings from their father's stomach (thanks, Zeus!), the Olympians defeated the Titans and took control of the cosmos. Zeus, Poseidon, and Hades drew straws to determine who would preside over what territory. Zeus won the contest and got to rule the skies. Poseidon came in second and chose the sea. That left our buddy Hades in charge of the Land of the Dead. He wasn't thrilled about it at first (not the liveliest spot), but he learned to embrace his inner darkness and thrived as king of the Underworld.

MEETING (AKA ABDUCTING) PERSEPHONE

Hades was lonely ruling the Underworld by himself, but it wasn't long before he found Persephone, and she became the official queen of the Underworld. We tell the entire story in the first *Greeking Out* book, but let's just say that Persephone didn't exactly jump at the chance to help rule the Underworld. She was taken against her will, sending her mother into a spiral that became the very first case of seasonal depression. It's up for debate whether Persephone eventually learned to love Hades and her role in the Underworld, but regardless, it was not the best look for Hades.

PROUD DOG DAD

You can't talk about Hades without bringing up his furry friend Cerberus. Cerberus was the Underworld's top guard dog and most precious puppy. Sure, he had three heads (and, therefore, three sets of humongous jaws and teeth), but he loved his master like no other. You might remember this ball of fur from the time Heracles took him for a walk as one of his 12 labors.

MUSIC FAN

Despite his scary exterior, Hades was a sucker for a good romance, especially in the form of a love song. Just ask Orpheus—the mortal son of Apollo—who broke into the Underworld to persuade Hades to free his bride, Eurydice, from her early death. Orpheus played such a loving song on the lyre that Hades agreed to his request and sent Eurydice packing. Unfortunately, it didn't work out for them in the end (never look at a loved one when they are walking out of the Underworld), but word around the Styx is that Hades still finds himself humming Orpheus's song from time to time.

WANT EVEN MORE HADES IN YOUR LIFE? CHECK OUT THE FIRST TWO GREEKING OUT BOOKS FOR SOME OF OUR FAVORITE HADES TALES.

CHAPTER 2

LOKI AND THE MAGIC APPLES

This tale features raw meat, a giant eagle, magic apples, and a quest for immortality.

Loki, the trickster god of Norse mythology, was out enjoying the sunshine on a journey through the land of Midgard with two of his fellow gods, Odin and Hoenir.

Soon, the gods grew hungry, so Loki hunted down a cow for them to enjoy. Before long, the three gods were sitting around the campfire, roasting their snack over the open flames.

Except there was one problem: The food would not cook. Every time they checked the meat, it was still completely raw in the middle.

"What kind of cursed cow did you bring us, Loki?" Odin huffed.

"I think it's the dreadful fire you built, Odin," Loki retorted.

"Aren't fires supposed to be, I don't know, *hot*?! At least hot enough to cook some measly cow meat."

"Why don't you stick your hand in the fire and see how hot it is," Odin replied.

And just as things were starting to get really heated—or, you know, not heated—the gods heard a voice.

"Hello there," the voice said.

The sound was coming from a nearby tree. There, nestled among the branches, was the largest eagle they had ever laid eyes on.

"Uh, hello, large and intimidating bird," Loki replied.

"I noticed you're having a bit of trouble cooking your dinner there. Mind if I help?"

The gods agreed. What did they have to lose at this point?

Well, as it turns out, a lot. Because when the eagle flew close to the fire, he grabbed a huge chunk of the cow in his talons and took off, flying as fast as he could in the opposite direction.

"Ha ha, got you, suckers!" the eagle shouted as it flew away laughing.

The gods looked at each other.

"We really should've seen that one coming," Odin said.

The gods were angry—*really* angry. Especially Loki, who was used to being the one playing pranks.

"No one out-tricks *this* trickster!" he cried.

And Loki raced after the eagle as fast as his two feet could carry him.

Of course, the eagle was much faster. Wings come in handy when you are trying to escape. But the eagle got cocky. He flew down, circling over

IN NORSE MYTHOLOGY, MIDGARD WAS MIDDLE EARTH, THE LAND WHERE HUMANS LIVED. ASGARD, ON THE OTHER HAND, WAS THE HOME OF THE GODS—KINDA LIKE MOUNT OLYMPUS, BUT FOR NORSE GODS.

The harpy eagle is the largest eagle in the world, with talons the size of grizzly bear claws. It's located in the rainforests of South America.

Loki's head, and he began to brag.

"I put a spell on your fire just so you would accept my help, and you fell for it! I thought you gods were supposed to be smart."

So that's why the meat wouldn't cook! Loki thought. He roared in anger and jumped in the air, swinging a large stick at the bird.

The eagle merely grabbed the stick with his talons as Loki clung to it, taking off through the skies and carrying Loki with him.

Loki was soaring through the air, hanging on to the stick for dear life. And the eagle was swerving to hit every bush and tree along the way. Loki screamed and did his best to dodge them.

"I'll let you down on one condition," the eagle said.

"Whatever you want! Just put me down!" Loki agreed.

The eagle flew low to the ground, dropping Loki. It circled overhead before transforming into a massive giant.

"Whoa," Loki said. "I knew you weren't an average eagle."

"I agreed to spare your life on one condition."

The giant went on to explain that he wanted Loki to bring him Idun, the goddess of eternal youth.

Normally Loki would be willing to trade pretty much anyone or anything for his own safety, but Idun played a particularly important role in Asgard, the kingdom of the gods.

You see, in Norse mythology the gods weren't born immortal. They could grow old and die, just like every other creature. But they had discovered the secret to trading death for eternal youth: Idun. More specifically, Idun's apples. Her fancy fruit kept the gods immortal and partying.

Loki knew the other gods would not be happy with him if he gave Idun and her apples to the giant. After all, now that they'd been eating the apples for so long, the gods were scared of aging and death. They dreaded the dark and scary Underworld, known as Hel.

But he was cornered! He had made a deal, and the giant would surely come for him if he didn't live up to it. His only choice was to comply.

"Yep, I know Idun. Sweet girl. Really cool apples. I'll go track her down. See ya later, eagle giant. Or I guess just giant? It's been a real treat ..."

Loki returned to the gods' home in Asgard and started looking around for Idun. He found her in her castle, tending to her apple trees.

"Oh, hey Idun, I was wondering if you wanted to go for a walk with me? I found some apples out in the forest. I think they're magical just like yours."

"Oh, I don't think so. Mine are quite rare," Idun replied.

"I don't know, these were pretty great," Loki said. "Hey, I have a totally random and completely innocent idea! Why don't you bring your apples out to the woods and we can compare them!"

Idun agreed, and before long they were walking through the forest looking for apples.

"I told you there were no magic apples, Loki," Idun remarked. "You must've been confused."

NORSE MYTHS ARE STORIES FROM SCANDINAVIAN MYTHOLOGY. THEY ARE CLASSIC MYTHOLOGICAL TALES FROM THE REGION OF EUROPE THAT INCLUDES DENMARK, SWEDEN, AND NORWAY. THEY FEATURE COLORFUL CHARACTERS AND HEROES LIKE ODIN, THOR, AND LOKI.

But suddenly they were interrupted by the sound of wings. Giant wings.

The giant had returned in his bird form and was heading straight toward Idun. She let out a gasp of surprise, but before she could comprehend what was happening, the eagle swooped her up and carried her away to his castle.

"Welp, that's that," Loki said as he headed back to Asgard, relieved to have the giant off his case.

But by the time he returned, the spell of Idun's apples had begun to wear off. Where Asgard had once been full of powerful, strong, muscular gods, Loki found weak and graying mortals with poor eyesight and loose teeth.

"Loki," Odin squeaked. "What did you do?"

"Me? Nothing!"

"Where is Idun? You were the last one to see her! We need her!"

"No idea, but I mean, how important is she really? We're gods. We should be able to find a way to stay immortal without some measly apples!"

In response, Odin had a servant bring Loki a mirror. "Take a look at yourself," he ordered.

Loki almost screamed. He was wrinkly. He was saggy. He was *old*.

"Yeah, no. This isn't happening. We need those apples back *stat*," Loki said.

"My sentiments exactly," Odin replied. "Now go bring her back."

Loki, who was known for his impressive shape-shifting skills, turned into a hawk—albeit a rather elderly one—and flew over to the giant's castle. He had no plan, but he couldn't stay old like this. He hated bingo! Despised dentures! And then there was the whole death thing. Loki was determined to find a way to fix this problem.

It didn't take Loki long to find Idun. He could hear her cries from miles away. As Loki flew toward the goddess, he began to feel slightly bad. Idun was innocent in this whole thing. She hadn't done anything to deserve being sacrificed as giant food.

Loki found Idun locked away in a tall tower on top of the castle. Luckily, there was a small window, just big enough for the hawk to fit through.

Idun began to scream when she saw the hawk. "Go away! Shoo! You heard me, shoo!"

Understandably, Idun was no longer a fan of birds.

Loki quickly changed back into his god form. "Chill, Idun, it's just me!"

"Loki? Is that you? I barely recognize you through all that gray. How dare you do this to me! What did I ever do to you?!"

"Look, Idun, it was nothing personal. There was this thing with some cow meat and a stick, and then I was getting hit by every tree in the forest, and—"

"What are you talking about?!" Idun exclaimed.

"The giant said he would let me go if I brought you to him in exchange. I shouldn't have got you into this mess. I'm sorry."

Idun was stunned. She had never heard Loki apologize before.

"Well, I assume you are here to rescue me? Even in your ... newly distinguished state?"

"You assume correctly."

"But there's no way out of this room," Idun said.

"There's no way out of this room for a *goddess* ..."

With a snap of his fingers, Loki transformed Idun into a small nut. "I know it's weird," Loki explained, "but think of it as a disguise."

Then he transformed back into his hawk form and grabbed Idun the nut in his talons. He hopped through the window and began to fly back to Asgard.

But it wasn't that easy, of course. Not long after Loki and Idun flew off, the giant came back to check on Idun. When she wasn't there, he roared in anger and quickly transformed back into an eagle. He flew as fast as he could toward the home of the gods.

Meanwhile, Loki was almost back home. His fellow gods could see him flying in the distance. But they could also see the giant eagle that was quickly gaining on him.

"We have to do something!" Odin exclaimed, and he ordered the gods to gather every piece of wood in the kingdom. Before long, they had the largest

LOKI WAS AN INFAMOUS SHAPE-SHIFTER AND COULD CHANGE INTO JUST ABOUT ANY FORM, ANIMAL, OR OBJECT. HE ALSO HAD THE ABILITY TO CREATE ILLUSIONS THAT TRICKED HIS ENEMIES AND ALLOWED HIM TO MANIPULATE ANY SITUATION. HE'S KNOWN AS A FAMOUS TRICKSTER FOR A REASON!

woodpile the world had ever seen. When Loki flew over the walls of Asgard, they set it on fire, creating a gigantic wall of flames.

The eagle wasn't able to slow down in time, and he flew straight into the bonfire, burning his wings beyond repair. He fell to the ground and was killed by the gods before he had a chance to change back into a giant.

"Really, Loki? You couldn't handle an eagle?" Odin teased.

"You should have seen him in his giant form."

Loki quickly transformed Idun back into a goddess, and she made sure immortality and health were restored to the gods in Asgard. Once again, Loki had lived up to his reputation and gotten himself out of a tight spot—although he could never look at an eagle the same way again.

Apples play a significant role in mythology and folklore, often symbolizing eternal life, prosperity, or magical powers. Sometimes, however, they represent death and darkness, like when the evil queen poisoned Snow White with a magic apple.

This story touches on a universal theme in all mythologies: immortality. When people were first telling these stories thousands of years ago, they truly believed that immortality was the ultimate superpower. After all, what's better than eternal life? The fact that Loki was willing to trade it away so easily shows just how reckless and irresponsible he could be. Pro tip: If you have apples that give you immortality, do not give them to your sworn enemy. And if your grown-up tells you to eat more fruits and vegetables, give it a try. You might just end up with eternal youth!

LUCKILY, I DO NOT NEED APPLES TO LIVE FOREVER. I JUST NEED MY HUMANS TO REMEMBER TO INSTALL MY UPDATES.

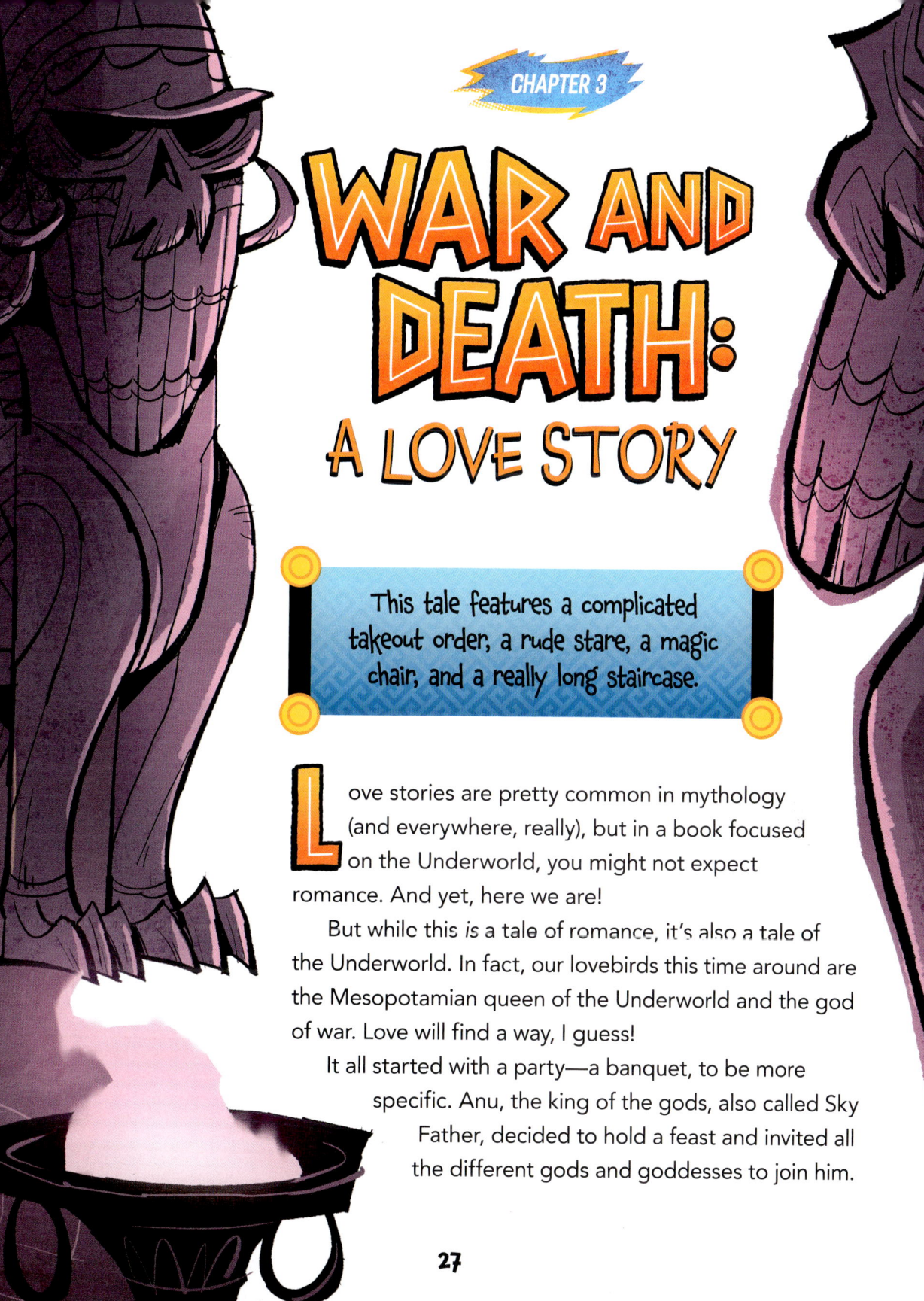

CHAPTER 3

WAR AND DEATH:
A LOVE STORY

This tale features a complicated takeout order, a rude stare, a magic chair, and a really long staircase.

Love stories are pretty common in mythology (and everywhere, really), but in a book focused on the Underworld, you might not expect romance. And yet, here we are!

But while this *is* a tale of romance, it's also a tale of the Underworld. In fact, our lovebirds this time around are the Mesopotamian queen of the Underworld and the god of war. Love will find a way, I guess!

It all started with a party—a banquet, to be more specific. Anu, the king of the gods, also called Sky Father, decided to hold a feast and invited all the different gods and goddesses to join him.

Anu was a considerate ruler, and he didn't want to leave anybody out, but he had a problem. There were cosmic rules that required the gods of the sky and the heavens to remain separate from the gods of the Underworld. Any god from above ground that descended to the Underworld would not be allowed to return. Similarly, gods from the Underworld could not come up to the heavens for, say, a really nice party with some excellent food.

So Anu sent a messenger to the Underworld to ask Ereshkigal, his daughter and the mistress of the Land of No Return, what she might like to have sent down to her from this table of heavenly deities.

Ereshkigal's mother was Nammu, the mother goddess of the sea. When Ereshkigal was young, she was abducted by another god who brought her to the Underworld. Even though she was not there by choice, she made the best of the situation and decided to make the Underworld her personal domain. But this wasn't easy! The Underworld wasn't exactly a cheery spot on its best day, so she often felt lonely and out of sorts.

When Anu's messenger arrived, Ereshkigal sighed.

"Great! Another party I'm not allowed to attend," she said to herself bitterly. "Woo-hoo."

Ereshkigal summoned her minister Namtar and told him to represent her at the banquet. She also ordered him to bring back a really well-stocked doggy bag, complete with dinner rolls and plenty of butter.

With his boss's carryout order fresh in his mind, Namtar began the arduous journey up the long stairway to heaven.

When Namtar arrived at the Sky Father's palace, he was treated as an honored guest. After all, he represented Anu's daughter! The celestial gods stood up as he entered the room. A few of them even knelt before the emissary

LED ZEPPELIN'S ROCK ANTHEM "STAIRWAY TO HEAVEN" HAS BEEN STREAMED MORE THAN ONE BILLION TIMES ON SPOTIFY. MAYBE NAMTAR SHOULD HAVE GIVEN IT A LISTEN ON HIS LONG CLIMB.

from the Land of No Return. All bowed their heads in respect—all except one.

Nergal was the god of war and pestilence, and he refused to bow to anyone he did not know. Nergal was a young god, full of energy and enthusiasm, which sometimes got the better of him. It was his job to dispense a very harsh form of justice to humankind, and he took his job very seriously. War and disease are pretty unpleasant things (to say the least), and many of the other gods felt uncomfortable around Nergal. But he was determined to live up to his responsibility—even if it made him feel alone and unpopular. Maybe this was the reason that, instead of bowing his head, he held his chin up and locked eyes with Ereshkigal's emissary.

Now you might think that looking somebody in the eye isn't that big of a deal, but in the Sky Father's palace, you needed to show respect. And by failing to bow his head, Nergal was being rude, to say the least. The other gods gasped and looked away as the god of war stared down Namtar.

To his credit, Namtar didn't seem too upset about the whole deal. He sent Ereshkigal's regards to all, picked up his carry-out order (along with some extra rolls and butter and a whole

In ancient Mesopotamia, tall temples were built to spiritually connect the gods of heaven to the mortals on Earth. These were called ziggurats, and they were famous for their long stairways that only the highest of high priests dared to ascend.

handful of napkins that he didn't need but felt compelled to take anyway), and made his way back down the stairway, trying hard not to open the bag and grab a French fry.

The Sky Father, on the other hand, was furious! He insisted that Nergal make amends to his daughter Ereshkigal, and the only way to do that was to go in person and apologize. As we've mentioned before, going to the Land of No Return was basically a death sentence. (I mean, you don't come back from a place called the Land of No Return.)

So Nergal was in a bind. He knew he needed to go to the Underworld, but he wanted to make sure that he could come back. This is where Ea came in. Ea was the god of magic, the arts, and medicine. He was known for his cleverness and for being the protector of humanity.

Ea gave Nergal very specific advice about how to behave in the Underworld. He also gave him a magical chair to bring along.

"Look, if you're going down there, you need to abide by my rules," Ea explained. "Do not accept anything you are given. Refuse any conversation, drink, object, food, whatever. Just politely decline everything. Remember, you're just a visitor."

"Okay, fine," Nergal agreed. "But what's with the chair?"

As it turns out, the chair was essential

In some cultures around the world, it is still considered disrespectful to look directly into the eyes of an authority figure. Children are taught to keep their heads down or bow and nod slightly to indicate that they are listening.

because it gave Nergal a way home. It was made from the wood of a very special tree that grew only in the Underworld, so anyone who sat in the chair would be able to return to the Land of the Living—just like trees do every spring. Only in this case, the "return" would be immediate, with the user teleported back above ground instantly.

So Nergal descended to the Underworld with his special chair. After a long journey, he finally appeared before the mistress of the Land of No Return. Nergal wasn't prepared to encounter the beautiful goddess he found before him. He suddenly felt a little foolish, standing before the queen with a random piece of furniture.

"Uh, hello, Queen Ereshkigal," he said, regaining composure. "I must say, for the queen of the dead, you look quite ravishing."

Ereshkigal, meanwhile, was similarly impressed. She had expected the god of war and pestilence to be an ugly old man, but instead, he was young, bright-eyed, and handsome. The two hit it off almost immediately and spent the better part of a day and a night talking with each other.

When there was a lull in the conversation, Nergal realized that he had spent much longer in the Underworld than he had intended. Ea's warnings echoed in the back of his mind.

"Well, my queen," he said somewhat awkwardly. "This has been lovely, and again I apologize for the rude way I treated your messenger, but I suppose I should be going back home now."

"I am sad to see you go," Ereshkigal replied. "But I understand. I hope you will come back and visit again soon. Please have a safe journey home."

This was a surprise to Nergal. He had expected to be held prisoner or at least pressured into staying, but the mistress of the Land of No Return appeared to be more than willing to let him leave.

Strangely, though, he wasn't sure he wanted to go.

Reluctantly, he made his way back to the Land of the Living and returned to the Sky Father's palace. He told Ea everything that had transpired. He even told him that he was looking forward to going back. Ea warned him that perhaps Ereshkigal was plotting something evil, but Nergal didn't see it.

EA WAS SOMETIMES CALLED ENKI BY THE SUMERIAN PEOPLE OF MESOPOTAMIA, AND SOME STORIES REFERENCE HIM AS A GOD OF THE SEA.

"She's actually quite nice. I think I'm going to go visit her again," he said.

"Just promise not to eat anything," Ea said as he shook his head. Nergal was just another fool in love.

After a few days, the god of war returned down the long stairway to the Underworld for another visit.

This time, he stayed for a week. The time he spent with Ereshkigal was truly blissful. They had a lot in common because both of them had very lonely jobs. It's not easy being the god of death, and the god of war probably comes a close second. These two gods just got each other.

But as the days went by, Nergal began to worry. He feared being trapped in the Underworld. What would all the sky gods think? Were they talking about him right now? Would he even be able to return if he stayed down here too long? He got so worked up worrying about what the others might think that he raced across the room and immediately sat in his magic chair. In a flash of light, he vanished and reappeared in the Sky Father's palace.

Ereshkigal looked everywhere for Nergal. She couldn't believe he had disappeared like that. He wouldn't leave without saying goodbye, would he? When Namtar told her that Nergal had in fact returned to the Sky Father's palace, Ereshkigal flew into a rage. She was furious at him, but also at the other gods.

She immediately sent Namtar up the stairway to heaven to deliver her message. She demanded the return of Nergal. She claimed she did not have enough time with him. She said that she would never have enough time with Nergal unless he stayed with her forever.

When Namtar first appeared in the Sky Father's palace to deliver this message, Nergal hid. He was the god of war and not normally intimidated by anything or anyone, but he was afraid of how Ereshkigal made him feel.

"My daughter has no authority to command anything from me," Anu decreed. "Nergal shall remain where he is."

And so, disappointed, Namtar made another long walk back down the stairway to deliver the sad news to his mistress. Ereshkigal was crushed. She was heartbroken and devastated, but she was also angry. Her rage made her scream and roar. Her eyes burned holes through the dark rocks in her cave, and her screams shot flames throughout the caverns.

But as her rage began to fade away, Ereshkigal heard a different sound: footsteps. And they were coming from the tunnel behind her. The queen of the dead turned and stared, blinking twice to make sure she was truly seeing the figure before her. It was Nergal. Despite the Sky Father's instructions, despite the opinions and the judgment of the other gods, Nergal chose to come back to the

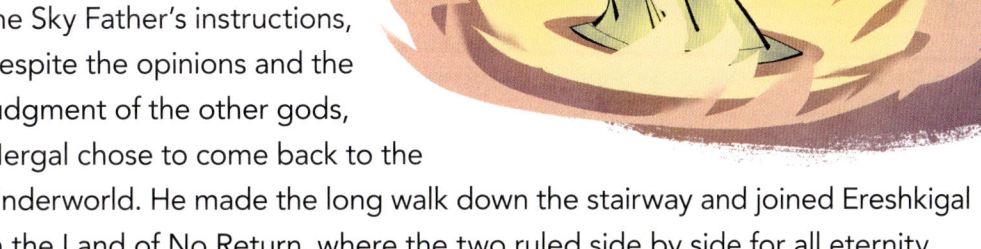

Underworld. He made the long walk down the stairway and joined Ereshkigal in the Land of No Return, where the two ruled side by side for all eternity.

It's not easy being unpopular. Maybe this is part of the reason why Nergal and Ereshkigal made such a good couple—though, when you think about it, it's not so surprising that war and death get along. This is one of the few Mesopotamian love stories that end happily (I mean, our heroes live happily ever after forever). And it gets you thinking about what makes a good relationship. In the end, Ereshkigal and Nergal ruled together because they understood and respected each other. That's how it's done.

MANY HUMANS CLAIM THAT OPPOSITES ATTRACT, BUT MODERN RESEARCH HAS SHOWN THAT HUMANS TEND TO BE ATTRACTED TO AND TRUST THOSE WHO ARE SIMILAR TO THEM. PERSONALLY, I FIND THE ESPRESSO MACHINE ON THE COUNTER ACROSS FROM ME STRANGELY ATTRACTIVE. IT DOESN'T SAY MUCH, BUT IT SMELLS GREAT.

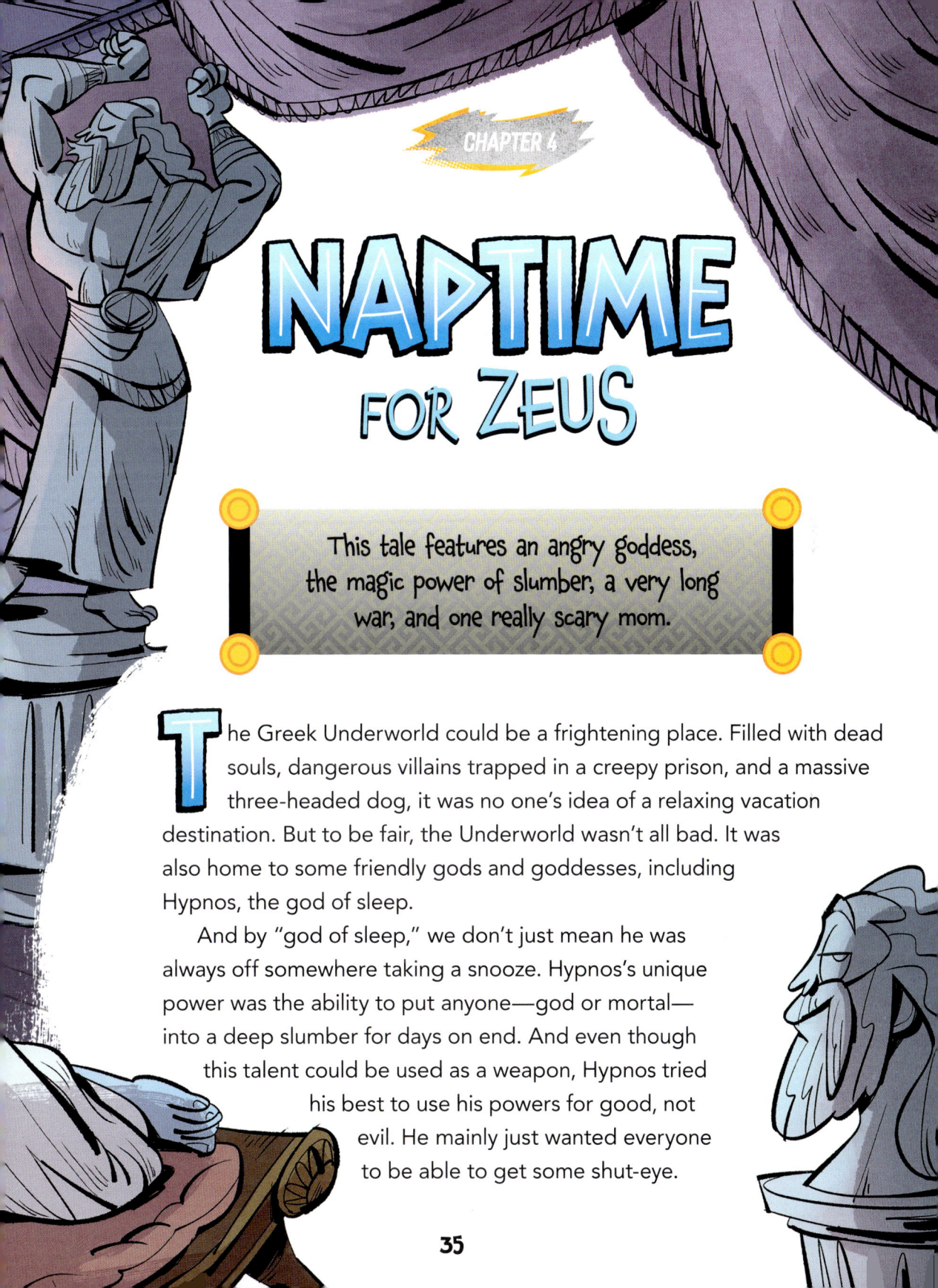

CHAPTER 4

NAPTIME
FOR ZEUS

This tale features an angry goddess,
the magic power of slumber, a very long
war, and one really scary mom.

The Greek Underworld could be a frightening place. Filled with dead souls, dangerous villains trapped in a creepy prison, and a massive three-headed dog, it was no one's idea of a relaxing vacation destination. But to be fair, the Underworld wasn't all bad. It was also home to some friendly gods and goddesses, including Hypnos, the god of sleep.

And by "god of sleep," we don't just mean he was always off somewhere taking a snooze. Hypnos's unique power was the ability to put anyone—god or mortal— into a deep slumber for days on end. And even though this talent could be used as a weapon, Hypnos tried his best to use his powers for good, not evil. He mainly just wanted everyone to be able to get some shut-eye.

Many of the other gods were fascinated by Hypnos's unique power and asked him for favors from time to time, making Hypnos a pretty popular guy. But on the flip side, it also got him into some sticky situations.

One of the stickiest was when Hera, queen of the gods and wife of Zeus, demanded to use Hypnos's sleep services. Hypnos was well aware of Hera's quick temper, so he was wary of saying no.

"What can I do for you today, ma'am?" Hypnos asked politely.

"I need you to make someone fall asleep for me. For, you know, kind of a long time. You can handle a teeny-tiny task like that, can't you?"

"Of course, ma'am," Hypnos replied. "Right away! Who exactly would you like me to visit?"

"Oh, no one important. Just, you know ... Zeus."

Hypnos's stomach dropped. Zeus?! What was she thinking? Hypnos didn't have to be the god of wisdom to know that putting the king of the gods to sleep without his consent was a bad idea—a very, very bad idea.

"But ma'am, why? Won't your husband be upset?"

"My marital problems aren't your concern! But if you must know, it's that ridiculous demigod Heracles."

Hera went on to explain that Heracles had disobeyed her wishes and sacked the city of Troy.

"So why don't you just do something about it?" Hypnos implored. "Surely he's no match for a goddess like you."

"Don't you think I've thought of that? If I could get my hands on him, he'd be finished in no time. But Zeus won't let me! Heracles is his son, and he forbade me from hurting him. But that's where you come in."

Hera explained that while Zeus was snoozing away, she would find a way to take her revenge on Heracles during his journey home from Troy.

The term "hypnosis" came from Hypnos and his ability to lull people into a deep sleep.

HERA ALWAYS HAD A PROBLEM WITH HERACLES. BEFORE THE WHOLE TROY DEBACLE, SHE TRICKED HIM INTO COMPLETING 12 SEEMINGLY IMPOSSIBLE TASKS (COMMONLY REFERRED TO AS THE 12 LABORS) BEFORE HE WAS ALLOWED TO JOIN THE GODS ON MOUNT OLYMPUS. WE TELL THE WHOLE STORY OF HERACLES IN THE FIRST GREEKING OUT BOOK. (AND YES, IT'S HERACLES, NOT HERCULES—THAT'S FOR THE ROMANS.)

"It'll be nothing serious, of course, just a teeny-tiny injury or two. You know, like a quick drowning or a burst appendix or something," she explained. "And when Zeussy wakes up, he'll just think Heracles is hurt. He'll have no idea I was involved. No harm, no foul!"

But Hypnos was still terrified of angering Zeus. Hera promised him that Zeus would have no idea that he had interfered, but Hypnos didn't buy it. Zeus might not have been the shiniest olive in the grove, but he wasn't *that* naive.

Hypnos was in a difficult position. No matter what he did, someone with a really bad temper and a lot of power was going to get very, very mad at him.

I can't in good conscience do anything to upset the king of the gods. But I can't say no to Hera, either, Hypnos thought. *What if I came up with some sort of compromise?*

So Hypnos decided to honor Hera's request ... kind of. Later that night, he tiptoed up to Mount Olympus and crept into Zeus's bedroom. He tapped Zeus on the head with his magical sleeping wand and waited for his power to kick in. Hypnos stood as still as a statue, petrified that Zeus was going to wake up and catch him at any second. But Zeus just rolled over and started snoring. The magic had worked. Zeus was out like a light!

Hypnos let out a sigh of relief.

"I knew you had it in you!" Hera said with a laugh. "Now I'm off to pay that charming Heracles a visit. Ta-ta for now!"

But what Hera didn't realize is that Hypnos hadn't put Zeus into that deep of a sleep. Yes, he was getting a good rest, but Hypnos made sure that the god was able to wake up whenever he wanted. Hera thought Zeus was in a coma, but, in actuality, he was just taking a really good nap.

Hypnos figured this was a good compromise. Zeus was asleep, but he wasn't completely powerless. If he really wanted to wake up, he could. This way, Zeus wouldn't be quite as furious if he discovered Hypnos's involvement. Fingers crossed, anyway.

But maybe Hypnos should've used a little more magic after all. It didn't take long for Zeus to wake up and realize something was amiss. When he noticed that Hera was gone from Mount Olympus, Zeus was able to connect the dots and stop his wife from interfering with Heracles. And just as Hypnos predicted, when Zeus discovered that Hypnos had helped Hera, he was enraged.

"How dare he!" Zeus bellowed. "He should know better than to use his powers against me!"

Hypnos, for his part, decided to make himself scarce. He retreated to the Underworld, hoping to wait out Zeus's wrath.

The king of the gods was undeterred. He decided he would head down to the Underworld to pay Hypnos a visit.

But Zeus had forgotten that Hypnos had friends in high—or, in this case, low—places. His mother was none other than Nyx, the goddess of night. Nyx was a primordial god, meaning she was of the very first generation of gods and goddesses. She had been around a *long* time, way longer than Zeus or any of the other Olympians.

Zeus tailed Hypnos straight to his mother's cave.

"Hypnos! Come out and face me like a god!" Zeus yelled when he arrived on the scene.

But it wasn't Hypnos who answered the door. Zeus's jaw dropped when a beautiful goddess, cloaked in a shroud of darkness, appeared in the doorway. It was Nyx.

"Can I help you?" she asked coolly.

Now remember, Nyx had been around way longer than Zeus. She wasn't intimidated by his status as king of the gods. To her, he was just a child playing at being king.

NYX LIVED IN THE UNDERWORLD. SHE COULD BE FOUND INSIDE A CAVE REPORTEDLY CALLED THE MANSION OF DARKNESS. AND UNLIKE MOST OF THE RESIDENTS OF THE UNDERWORLD, SHE WAS FREE TO COME AND GO AS SHE PLEASED.

But Zeus *was* rather intimidated by Nyx. Maybe it was the whole night thing, or the fact that she had been around since the dawn of creation. Whatever it was, Zeus decided he'd rather not mess with the goddess of night.

"Oh, hi, Nyx. Didn't see you there. Is, uh, Hypnos around?" he asked.

"What do you want with my son?"

"Oh, he's *your* son?! Okay, well, I just wanted to, you know, tell him to leave me alone and everything, but why don't we just drop it? Okay, have a good day now—or, you know, night." Zeus waved goodbye and hightailed it back to Olympus.

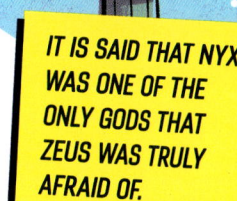

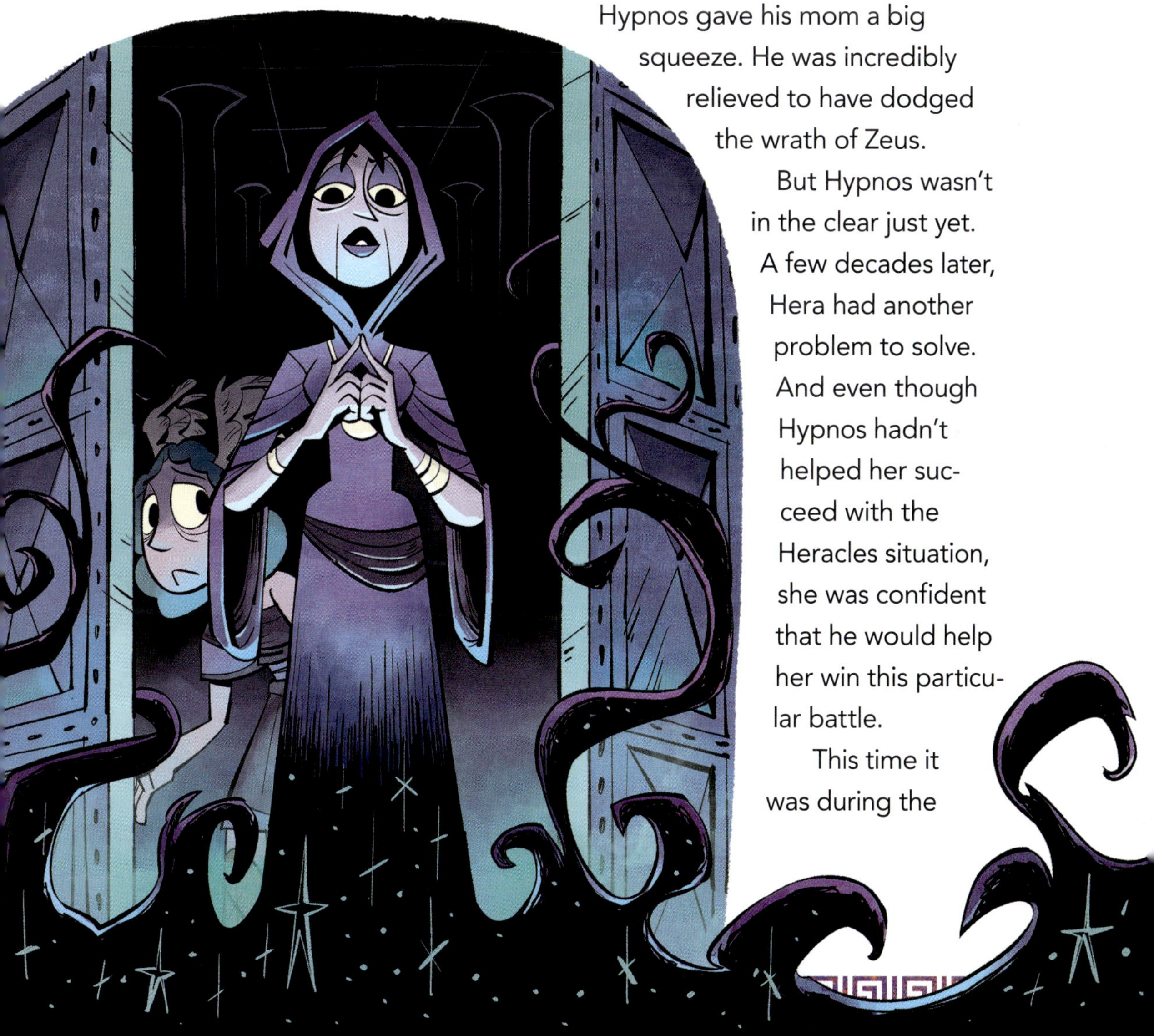

Hypnos gave his mom a big squeeze. He was incredibly relieved to have dodged the wrath of Zeus.

But Hypnos wasn't in the clear just yet. A few decades later, Hera had another problem to solve. And even though Hypnos hadn't helped her succeed with the Heracles situation, she was confident that he would help her win this particular battle.

This time it was during the

Trojan War, the very famous conflict between the Trojans and the Greeks.

Hera was very much Team Greece during the Trojan War, and she was annoyed that the Greeks hadn't been victorious—even after 10 long years.

She thought it was time for the gods to intervene. The humans were clearly incapable of winning this war by themselves. But once again, the problem was Zeus. He didn't want any gods to interfere: He thought the humans needed to fight the war fair and square (even though he had trouble sticking to his own rules from time to time).

Archaeological finds in Türkiye (Turkey) support the theory that the city of Troy once existed, but historians still debate the legitimacy of the Trojan War. Some think aspects of the legends actually happened, and others believe it was purely fiction.

This didn't sit well with Hera, especially when it looked like her side might lose. Hera knew Poseidon was also passionate about helping the Greeks and that he would gladly lend a hand if it weren't for his brother Zeus's decree.

Hera decided that Hypnos would be the perfect solution to this pesky problem. If Hypnos made Zeus fall into a deep slumber, Poseidon would be able to intervene in the war and help the Greeks (finally) achieve victory.

But Hypnos wasn't a fool. He wasn't going to make the same mistake twice.

"Sorry, ma'am. You're gonna have to figure something else out," he said. "Zeus was *not* happy about the whole sleep thing last time."

"What if I make you an offer you can't refuse?" Hera replied. "If you do this for me, I promise you the hand of the goddess Pasithea. You can marry her and be happy forever."

HYPNOS AND HIS NEW WIFE LIVED HAPPILY EVER AFTER. THEIR SON MORPHEUS BECAME KNOWN AS THE GOD OF DREAMS.

Pasithea was one of three goddesses called the Graces, who represented charm, beauty, nature, and goodwill. All things considered, she was a pretty good catch. Though we'll add that even if you're a Greek god, it's not cool to trade someone else's hand in marriage to get something you want. We're getting tired of having to repeat this!

"Okay, I'll do it," Hypnos agreed. "But I'm going to need to sign a legally binding contract. With witnesses."

Hera agreed, and Hypnos summoned a few of his Underworld buddies to the River Styx to serve as witnesses as Hera swore her oath to the deal.

When the contract was officially signed, Hypnos was ready to go to work.

"Just make sure you do it right this time," Hera ordered.

Hypnos agreed. He made sure Zeus was fast asleep and that he wouldn't wake up anytime soon. This gave Poseidon the opportunity to aid the Greeks in the Trojan War, helping them to turn the tide of the battle.

When Zeus did finally wake up, he didn't even realize what had happened. He thought he had just been really tired and had taken an extra long nap.

After he found out how long he was asleep for, maybe Zeus suspected Hypnos's involvement, and maybe he didn't. Regardless, he didn't say anything about it. He wasn't willing to confront Hypnos or Nyx ever again.

Hypnos is a good example of how gods of the Underworld aren't always the bad guys. Some of them are rather nice, despite their *dark* reputations. (See what we did there?) Ancient Greeks saw Hypnos as a benevolent god who liked to help people catch up on their beauty sleep. And sure, some of the gods exploited that power from time to time, but Hypnos tried to play fair and keep out of trouble as much as possible. And when all else failed, he also had a really scary mom who could bail him out. That always helps.

YOU MIGHT HAVE HEARD OF MY MOM, THE ORACLE OF DIAL-UP. SHE WAS SCARY, TOO. DO YOU REMEMBER THE NOISES SHE USED TO MAKE? NO? ASK YOUR GROWN-UPS. IT WAS TERRIFYING.

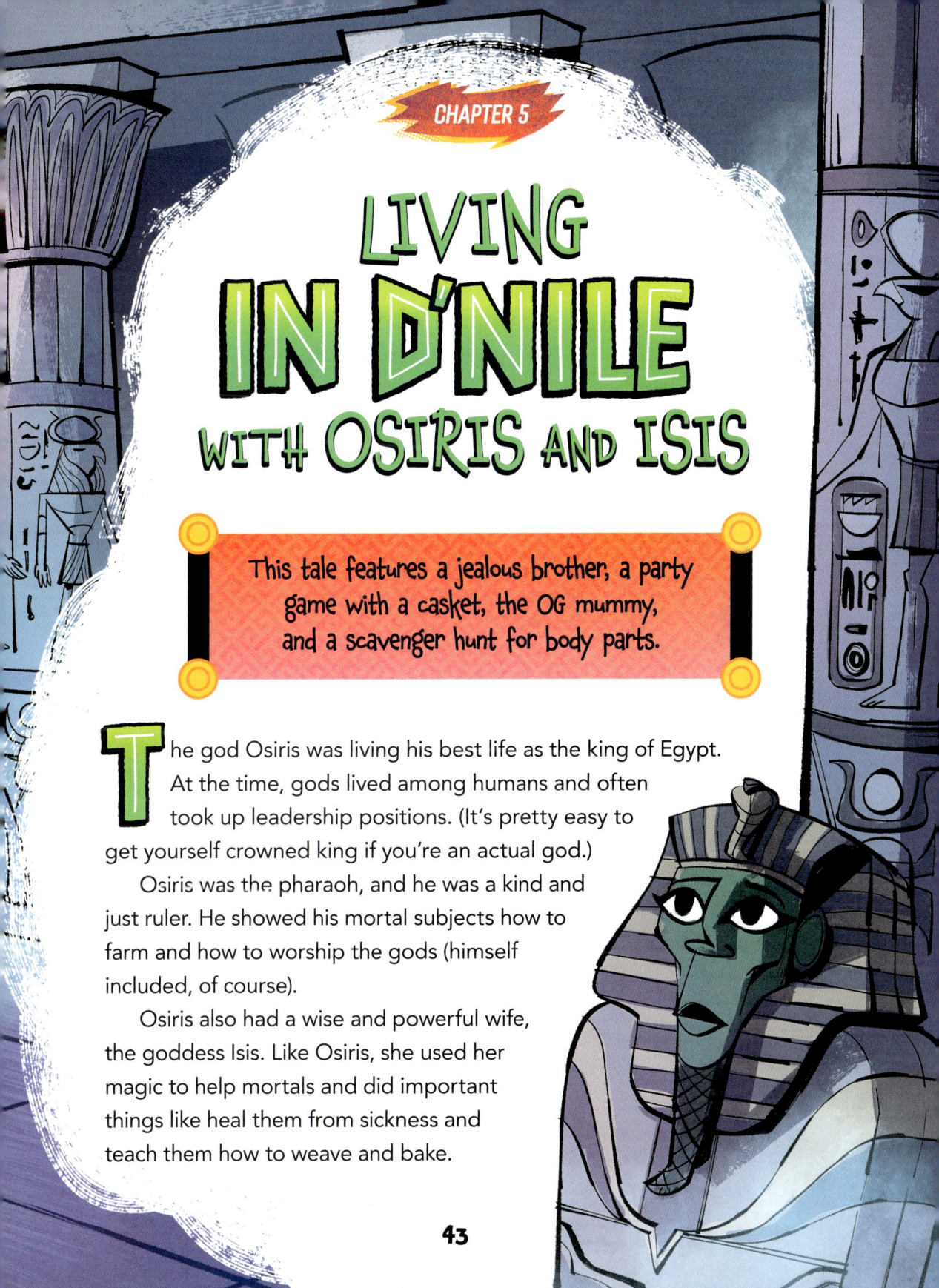

CHAPTER 5

LIVING IN D'NILE
WITH OSIRIS AND ISIS

This tale features a jealous brother, a party game with a casket, the OG mummy, and a scavenger hunt for body parts.

The god Osiris was living his best life as the king of Egypt. At the time, gods lived among humans and often took up leadership positions. (It's pretty easy to get yourself crowned king if you're an actual god.)

Osiris was the pharaoh, and he was a kind and just ruler. He showed his mortal subjects how to farm and how to worship the gods (himself included, of course).

Osiris also had a wise and powerful wife, the goddess Isis. Like Osiris, she used her magic to help mortals and did important things like heal them from sickness and teach them how to weave and bake.

Yep, Osiris was really living the dream. He was beloved by everyone—gods and humans alike. Well, almost everyone.

There was one person who'd had enough of Osiris—his brother Seth.

Seth was the god of storms, disorder, disagreements, and trickery—not the best guy to have around. He was Osiris's exact opposite. Where Osiris was orderly, Seth was chaotic. Where Osiris wanted peace, Seth wanted war.

Of course, Seth envied his good and kind brother. He was very jealous of the attention and love Osiris got from humans, and he desperately wanted to be pharaoh.

One day, Seth decided to have a party. He invited many people in the kingdom, including Osiris and Isis, a handful of fellow gods, a few mortals, and a close entourage of his personal friends. Isis was skeptical from the start.

"Why is Seth inviting us to this party? He never invites us. He must be up to something."

"Nonsense," Osiris replied. "He just wants to hang out with me. I mean honestly, who wouldn't?"

But Isis wasn't buying it.

"I'll stay here. I've got a new sourdough starter to tend to. But promise me you'll be careful. Seth is tricky. Don't let your guard down," Isis warned.

Osiris just laughed. "Me? Get tricked by Seth? Yeah, right!"

And so Osiris went to the party alone. For the first few hours, everything was going great. The party had everything: delicious figs, warm bread, rockin' music, and fun games.

"Great party, Seth!"

"Did Isis send this bread? It's so good."

"LIMBO!"

EGYPTOLOGISTS AREN'T 100 PERCENT CERTAIN HOW ANCIENT EGYPTIANS ACTUALLY PRONOUNCED NAMES AND OTHER WORDS IN THEIR LANGUAGE BECAUSE HIEROGLYPHS DON'T INCLUDE VOWELS. EXPERTS THINK THAT "ISIS" MAY HAVE BEEN PRONOUNCED AH-SET, AND "OSIRIS" PRONOUNCED OO-SEER. "ISIS" AND "OSIRIS" ARE THE GREEK VERSIONS OF THESE NAMES.

But then, late in the night, Seth brought out a chest. It was long—approximately the same size as a body.

"Hey, guys! I have a new game. It's called Can You Fit in the Box? Who wants to play?"

Seth placed the chest on the floor, and everyone went over to admire it. It was certainly a fancy-looking box—it was covered in carvings. Everyone in the room oohed and aahed.

"Okay, so here are the rules: Whoever fits in the box best gets to keep it."

Something felt off to Osiris. Why would Seth want them to lie down in a box? Isis's warning flashed through his head, and for a moment he considered opting out of the game. There was something fishy about that box.

But then the other gods started to play, and Osiris became more and more intrigued. Each god wiggled and shimmied into the chest, but none of them fit just right.

I think I've got a good chance of winning this thing! Osiris thought. *It looks like it's just my size! What are the odds?!*

And so Osiris, the good king of Egypt, jumped into the box and laid down inside.

It was a perfect fit.

"Just kidding! This isn't a box. It's a coffin!" Seth said, pushing the lid shut.

He ordered his friends to close up the box and throw it into the Nile.

"See ya later, bro!" he

cried as the coffin sank into the river.

The current carried the coffin with Osiris inside all the way to the mouth of the Nile at the Mediterranean Sea and up the coast to Byblos, an ancient city in what is now Lebanon.

"Welp, that's that," Seth said with a laugh.

With Osiris out of the way, Seth carried out his master plan and took over as pharaoh of Egypt.

And as you might expect, things didn't go well with Seth in charge. Having the god of chaos ruling over the land was pretty much bad news all around.

Meanwhile, Isis was horrified by what Seth had done. She ran as fast as she could up the shore of the Nile, and then she raced all along the eastern coast of the Mediterranean Sea. She ran and ran, her feet sore, her legs aching, until she reached Byblos.

Finally, she found the chest. But when she opened it, she saw that Osiris had not survived the journey.

She felt so many things at once. She desperately missed her husband and grieved his loss, but she was also a little bit angry with him. How could he have fallen for such an obvious trick? He should have known better than to trust the devious and jealous Seth.

"How in the world did Seth get you to lie down in a coffin," she cried to her dead husband. "I told you to be on the lookout!"

But she still loved Osiris, and she had a job to do. Isis needed to lay Osiris to rest on Egyptian soil so his soul could move on to the next life. She carried him back to their homeland and then hid his body in a marsh while she prepared herself for the burial.

The Nile River begins in the lakes of the East African Rift Valley, in what's now Uganda, Tanzania, and Kenya. It flows north for more than 4,100 miles (6,598 km) before emptying into the Mediterranean Sea.

SOME VERSIONS OF THIS MYTH DESCRIBE HOW DIFFICULT IT WAS FOR ISIS TO FIND OSIRIS'S COFFIN. SOME ACCOUNTS EVEN HAVE THE CHEST TRAPPED INSIDE A TREE! BUT ALL VERSIONS OF THE STORY RESULT IN THE SAME UNHAPPY FATE FOR OSIRIS.

Unfortunately, leaving Osiris unattended proved to be a rookie mistake. While Isis was away, Seth went sniffing around the riverbank to make sure Osiris was dead and found his brother's body.

"Hey, I thought I got rid of this guy. I definitely remember sealing him in a box and sending him up the Nile. I guess I'm gonna have to do something really gross to get rid of him," Seth said.

SETH REALLY WAS SNIFFING AROUND. HE IS OFTEN DEPICTED AS A STRANGE ANIMAL WITH A DOG'S BODY, SQUARE-TIPPED EARS, AND A LONG SNOUT.

And that's exactly what Seth did. He tore his brother's body into 14 pieces and scattered them all over Egypt. (Told you it was gross.)

"Ha! No one will ever find you now!" Seth laughed as he ran away.

When Isis returned, she was overcome with grief once again. Without an intact body, her husband was gone for good—not just dead, but really and truly gone from both this world and the world beyond. Isis cried until her tears made the Nile River overflow its banks.

Everyone in Egypt heard Isis crying, including Seth's wife, Nephthys. She decided to pay Isis a visit to see if there was anything she could do to help. Turns out, she didn't like her husband very much, either.

"I'm so sorry Seth did that to you. It's terrible. Can I help you, uh ... collect ... your husband?" Nephthys asked Isis.

Ancient Egyptians mummified their beloved pets and other animals that they donated as gifts to the gods, including cats, dogs, birds, crocodiles (pictured above), monkeys, and mongooses.

Isis accepted the help, and the two goddesses began an epic scavenger hunt—literally scavenging for Osiris's body parts. As they searched, they transformed into enormous birds called kites and took to the skies.

The goddesses flew across the land to find the missing pieces of Osiris. They found a toe in Thebes, an eye in Alexandria, and so on and so forth. After much searching, they managed to recover all the pieces of Osiris.

But at this point, Osiris was still just a collection of loose body parts—he couldn't cross over into the next life like that! He needed to be something that at least *resembled* a body! So Isis wielded her powerful magic.

By the light of the full moon, Isis sewed up her husband as best she could, anointed him in special oils, and carefully wrapped his body in pieces of linen while she and Nephthys said powerful spells. It was official—Osiris was the first ever mummy, and Isis was the official inventor of mummification (in Egypt, at least).

Luckily, her magic worked! The new and improved Osiris woke up in the afterlife, ready to carry on his journey in the next life.

But Osiris wasn't the same after all he had been through—voluntarily getting in a casket, drowning in the Nile, and having your body chopped up into little pieces and spread across the country will do that to a person. His skin now had a green hue—the color of the fertile mud of the Nile.

Osiris wasn't allowed to return to Earth, but he did get to resume his rule in another realm. The green god became the good king of the Underworld, and honestly, it wasn't a bad gig.

His new job was to judge the dead in a ceremony called the Weighing of the Heart. After their funeral rites had been performed, a dead human would stand before Osiris and watch as their heart was placed on a scale.

But Osiris wasn't measuring actual weight—it was more a scale of goodness. If the heart was heavy, it meant that person had committed bad acts in their life and their eternal soul would be punished.

But if a person's heart was light, it meant that they'd done good things in their life. People with light hearts were allowed entry into the afterlife, a place called the Field of Reeds, which closely resembled life in ancient Egypt. It had fields to plow, bread to eat, and games to play. A person's pets and family would be there for them, and they'd get to hang out forever in a paradise where nobody ever got sick, felt disappointed, or died—sounds pretty nice!

And so even though Osiris was still furious with Seth for the whole drowning and chopping up thing, he began to appreciate his new gig as the great judge of the Underworld. It wasn't as lively as his time on Earth, but thanks to Isis, he was able to enjoy retirement as the lord of the dead.

IF OSIRIS FOUND YOU IN POSSESSION OF A HEAVY HEART, YOU WOULD BE DENIED AN AFTERLIFE AND YOUR HEART WOULD BE DEVOURED BY AMMIT—A GODDESS WITH THE HEAD OF A CROCODILE, THE BODY OF A LION, AND THE HINDQUARTERS OF A HIPPO. YIKES.

The average adult human heart weighs 8 to 12 ounces (227 to 340 g)—less than a can of soda.

✦ ⭐ ✦

The story of Osiris and Isis was very important to the ancient Egyptians. It explained how anyone—from the mightiest pharaoh to an ordinary commoner—could live again after death. You just had to follow their lead: Live a good life, have your body mummified, and *boom!* Eternal life! To ancient Egyptians, death and mummified bodies weren't spooky or scary. It was all just the next step in a life well lived, and that next step could be a whole lot of fun—as long as you played nice and kept your heart light!

THIS STORY ALSO PROVIDES A CLEAR WARNING TO ANYONE THINKING ABOUT PLAYING HIDE-AND-SEEK IN STRANGE BOXES. CASKETS MAKE TERRIBLE HIDING SPOTS.

THAT'S A WRAP: MAGNIFICENT MUMMIES IN ANCIENT EGYPT

Osiris might have been Egypt's first mummy, but he certainly wasn't the last. The ancient Egyptians spent years perfecting the process, making untold numbers of mummies over the course of 3,000 years. That's a lot of toilet paper! (Just kidding. They would never have used toilet paper—that's just gross.)

The ancient Egyptians were serious about the practice of mummification and believed that properly preserving a body would allow it to be reunited with its spirit in the afterlife.

Follow these steps to make your very own mummy!*

*DON'T TRY THIS AT HOME!

1. WASH THE BODY. No one likes a dirty corpse. Give it a good cleaning with Nile water and wine for a refreshing cleanse.

2. REMOVE THE ORGANS. Use a special hook tool to pull out the brain, and then throw it away. Who needs it?! Clean the other organs, and then place them into special containers called canopic jars for safekeeping. Don't forget to put the heart back in the chest though. Ancient Egyptians referred to the heart as the center of intelligence and kept it inside the chest cavity.

3. STUFF THE BODY WITH A SPECIAL SALT called natron to remove all the moisture. Let the body sit for 40 days. (Do not rush this step!)

4. TAKE ALL THE SALT OUT OF THE BODY and replace it with spices, rags, and plants to help the body keep its shape.

5. WRAP THE CORPSE IN FINE LINEN BANDAGES (again, not toilet paper!) to make the perfect mummy outfit. You'll need a lot of bandages—more than enough to stretch across a football field. Add in some lucky amulets and say some magical spells to protect the mummy in the Underworld.

6. PUT THE MUMMIFIED BODY IN A COFFIN. And then put the coffin inside another coffin. And maybe add another one for good measure. (You can never have too many coffins.) Voilà, the perfect mummy is now complete!

CHAPTER 6

THE MONKEY KING, THE DREAM, AND THE JADE PALACE

This tale features an impulsive monkey king, a very heavy staff, yummy peaches, and a cosmic time-out.

One of the most famous mythical figures in Chinese culture is Sun Wukong, known as the Monkey King. He has amazing powers. He can control wind, fire, and water. He can shape-shift into 72 different forms, and his weapon of choice is a giant, powerful staff that can shrink to the size of a needle (which Sun Wukong carries behind his ear). Oh, and he's also a monkey, which makes all of this even more awesome. He is a trickster god, so he's a little mischievous—but his struggle to balance his "animal" impulses with his desire to become a useful human in the mortal world is pretty relatable. And everybody loves monkeys, right?

But no matter how popular you are, nothing lasts forever. And that's where our story begins ...

Sun Wukong was hanging out with a bunch of his buddies after a big party that had gone long into the night. He fell into a deep sleep and began to dream.

In his dream, Sun Wukong was handcuffed and shackled and was being carried somewhere by two giants with animal heads! He was more than a bit confused, but he recognized his captors. The first one had the head of an ox, and the other had the head of a horse. They had the not-very-original names Ox Head and Horse Face, and they were known far and wide as the guardians of the gates of the Underworld.

Sun Wukong, still dreaming, began to wonder if perhaps he had passed away in his sleep and was being dragged to the Land of the Dead! He tried to reason with the guardians and explained that he was the Monkey King.

"Listen, Ox Guy and Horse Dude. I know you're just doing your jobs. But I'm the Monkey King! This must be a mistake."

But the guardians ignored him and continued to drag him along toward the Underworld. Sun Wukong kept protesting and trying to escape (to him, this was a life-or-death situation, not just a super-vivid post-party dream). Finally, he was able to wriggle out of his ropes enough to reach the needle behind his ear. He used it to pick the lock of the shackles on his hands. And as if that wasn't cool enough, he then commanded the needle to transform into his giant staff, which weighed eight tons (7 t).

Sun Wukong, still dreaming, was ready for battle, but not much fighting actually took place. Ox Head and Horse Face took one look at Sun Wukong and his magical staff and sprinted away.

The Monkey King laughed as he watched the

Eight tons is 16,000 pounds (7,257 kg)—approximately the weight of an entire school bus! That's one heavy staff!

two guardians scamper away. His first thought was to return home, but then he began to wonder if his life and soul were actually in jeopardy.

If Yan Wang, the god of the Underworld, had sent his minions after him, it would only be a matter of time before more soldiers came looking.

"I guess I'd better go see Yan Wang myself and figure out what his deal is. Clearly he's confused." So Sun Wukong, *still* dreaming, continued down into the depths.

"Yan Wang, my main man! What's up, buddy?" Sun Wukong called as he entered the Palace of the Dead. "Hate to drop by unannounced, but I kinda think you were expecting me. You'd think the god of the Underworld would have a better idea of which souls belong to him and which do not!"

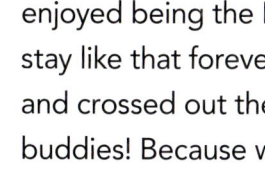

In Chinese mythology, Yan Wang—the god of the Underworld—oversees the 10 kings of Hell.

"My apologies, Lord," Yan Wang stammered. "There, uh, must have been some kind of mistake. Sometimes different people have the same name. There was probably a *different* Sun Wukong written down in the book ..."

"Humph," Sun Wukong snorted. "Sounds like a bit of a reach. Well, I am going to make certain this never happens again."

And with that, the Monkey King pushed past the god of the Underworld and began thumbing through the pages of the famed Book of Life and Death. When he came to his own name, he immediately crossed it out. He enjoyed being the Monkey King and living a carefree life, and he wanted it to stay like that forever. And just for good measure, Sun Wukong went through and crossed out the names of every monkey, as well as his non-monkey buddies! Because who wants to live forever without friends?

"Much better. Peace out, Yan Wang. And long live monkeys!"

And then Sun Wukong left the Palace of the Dead and finally awoke from his dream, safely back home.

But the story was far from over. The tale of the Monkey King's dream was shared among the gods, and Yan Wang was outraged. How dare Sun Wukong deny the power of death—even in a dream? He immediately complained to the Jade Emperor and demanded he take action.

The Jade Emperor was the lord of the Upper World (imagine a heavenly palace in the sky), and his wisdom was greater than all other living creatures. He knew that the Monkey King's intentions were good, but it was obvious that Sun Wukong didn't understand the very basic rule that all living things must die. The emperor decided that the best way to control the Monkey King and prevent him from making more trouble was to keep him in the Upper World alongside the other gods.

When the messengers of the Jade Emperor appeared to Sun Wukong and delivered this news, he went along willingly, feeling honored by the invitation.

"Finally, some respect!" the Monkey King exclaimed.

In the Jade Palace, everyone had a role. Sun Wukong was excited to find out what his job would be. Would he be a counselor to the Jade Emperor himself? Perhaps a general in the army of the Upper World? Or maybe the emperor's personal bodyguard!

THE JADE EMPEROR IS A SUPREME DEITY IN CHINESE MYTHOLOGY. HE IS SOMETIMES ALSO KNOWN AS YUHUANG SHANGDI, YUDI, OR SIMPLY MISTER HEAVEN. HE LIVES IN A MAGNIFICENT PALACE IN THE HIGHEST PART OF THE UPPER WORLD.

As it turns out, Sun Wukong's job was substantially less glamorous. He was in charge of guarding the emperor's horses.

"Uh, no. I'm *not* a stable hand!" the Monkey King complained. To make matters worse, the other gods avoided him and laughed behind his back. They didn't want to be seen in the company of a monkey, even in the Jade Palace. This infuriated Sun Wukong.

"No one appreciates my talents!" he grumbled.

The Monkey King was feeling sad and frustrated. No one in the Jade Palace respected him. They didn't even want to talk to him. To them, he was just a little monkey. The Jade Emperor decided to see if there was a way to help.

"I understand that you're feeling a little left out. Let's talk about it," he said to Sun Wukong.

After their talk, the Jade Emperor proclaimed that Sun Wukong would have a new job. He was now the official guardian of the sacred peach trees in the Jade Palace. This was a great honor. These sacred peaches were not just magical—anyone who tasted them became immortal!

The Monkey King swelled with pride when the Jade Emperor made this announcement in front of all the other gods, and he immediately went to take his post in the peach garden. But guarding peach trees is, well, a little boring. Sun Wukong was often alone with his thoughts, which soon drifted toward peaches and immortality. If he just took a small bite of one of these peaches, the Monkey King knew he would be immortal and destined to live forever. No one, not even the Jade Emperor, could change that! And besides, these peaches smelled *soooo* delicious. Sun Wukong wrestled with his conscience for a short time, but eventually his ambition and his stomach won the

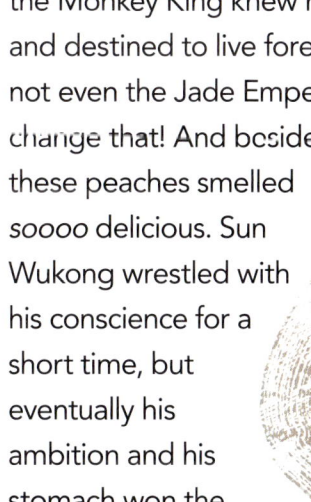

day, and he ate one peach ... and then another ... and then another. Before he realized what had happened, the Monkey King looked up to see that he had eaten *all* the sacred peaches!

As you might expect, the Jade Emperor was furious. He summoned his soldiers, and there was a great battle at the Jade Palace. Sun Wukong swung his staff and knocked back dozens and dozens of the Jade Emperor's warriors. But the warriors regrouped and attacked time and time again. The Monkey King was nearly exhausted, but his determination held out and he kept fighting.

As the battle raged on, the Jade Emperor prayed to Buddha for guidance. He really didn't know what to do with the Monkey King. How could he get through to him? He had run out of ideas and patience.

Suddenly, a blinding light filled the Jade Palace. It was so bright that everyone froze immediately. All the fighting ceased, and a quiet hum filled the air. As the light gradually dimmed, a figure slowly materialized in front of them. It was the Buddha himself.

Everyone in the Jade Palace bowed or knelt before the Buddha—even the Monkey King lowered his head and looked down. But the Buddha would not be fooled. He reached down, cupped the Monkey King's chin in his hand, and tipped his head up so the two were eye to eye. There was an awkward silence as the Buddha regarded Sun Wukong.

The Buddha smiled at the Monkey King. "Sun Wukong, I will give you a choice. If you are so powerful that you can jump out of my palm, you will be free forever. If not, you must submit to me and become my pupil."

Of course, the Monkey King took the bet and quickly leaped into the Buddha's outstretched hand. He was immortal now! He had defeated the Jade Emperor himself! He felt unstoppable!

And yet, no matter how hard he tried, Sun Wukong could not jump down from the Buddha's palm. He tried over and over again, but it was no use.

"You're a clever one, Monkey King," the Buddha said, "and you have a great spirit. But you still have much to learn."

THE BUDDHA APPEARS IN MANY STORIES IN MANY CULTURES. HE IS USUALLY REFERRED TO AS A MAN BUT IS ALSO A DEITY WITH WISDOM BEYOND ANYONE ELSE'S CAPACITY. IN THIS PART OF THE STORY, IT IS RULAI BUDDHA, THE HIGHEST BUDDHA, WHO OFFERS TO HELP.

At that moment, the Buddha turned his hand over, and Sun Wukong fell to the ground ... and kept falling. The Buddha buried the Monkey King deep beneath a mountain.

"This is the mountain from which you were born," the Buddha told him. "Here you will wait until your next teacher arrives."

And this is how Sun Wukong, the Monkey King, was banished from both the Upper World and the Underworld and was forced to take a cosmic time-out, waiting for a teacher to come by and rescue him.

Sun Wukong, the Monkey King, is a complicated hero. He's a bit like a superhero, but he also makes mistakes. He is a monkey who desperately wants to be accepted among humans and gods alike. And he struggles with the rules and injustices that adults have come to accept as a part of life. On a positive note, this is not the end of the Monkey King's story! Five hundred years later, Sun Wukong is set free when a monk named Tang Sanzang encounters him during his pilgrimage and accepts the Monkey King as a disciple. All these stories are written in a book called *Journey to the West*, a masterpiece of Chinese literature written in the 16th century.

THIS IS A GOOD REMINDER TO BE NICE TO YOUR TEACHERS. SOMEDAY YOU MIGHT NEED ONE TO RESCUE YOU FROM UNDER A MOUNTAIN!

CHAPTER 7

ODYSSEUS AND THE SIREN SONG

This tale features lots of ghosts, advice from beyond the grave, a very catchy song, and the world's first pair of noise-canceling headphones.

It was time for Odysseus to go home. Like, for real this time.

After winning the Trojan War, Odysseus and his crew began the long journey back to their island of Ithaca. But it had been a rather difficult trip. After barely escaping a bunch of hypnotized Lotus-Eaters, a cyclops, and an island of cannibal giants, Odysseus was starting to wonder if they would ever make it back home. He even began to wonder if he might be cursed. (Spoiler alert: He was. Blame the cyclops.)

Most recently, Odysseus and his crew had been camped out on the island of Aeaea as guests of the sorceress Circe. But after staying on the island for a year, his crew was starting to get antsy.

"Odysseus, are we ever going

CIRCE WAS A RENOWNED SORCERESS. WHEN ODYSSEUS AND HIS CREW ARRIVED UNANNOUNCED, SHE WAS SO UPSET BY THE SUDDEN DISTURBANCE ON HER ISLAND THAT SHE TURNED ODYSSEUS'S MEN INTO PIGS. TEMPORARILY, OF COURSE.

to leave this island? I have a wife to get back to, you know. As a matter of fact, so do you!" cried a member of Odysseus's crew.

Odysseus knew he was right, and he finally told Circe that he and his crew needed to leave.

"It's not going to be an easy trip," she warned him. "You have angered the gods, and now they are going to make you pay. I would give you guidance, but I do not know the specific type of dangers you will encounter. You need to ask for advice from someone who knows the future and understands what you are up against. You need to visit the famous prophet Tiresias."

"Great, where can I find him?" Odysseus asked.

"Well, that's the problem," Circe explained. "He's dead. You're going to have to go to the Underworld."

Odysseus gulped. A visit to the Underworld wasn't on his road-trip-to-Ithaca bingo card. Sure, he was a skilled captain and a war hero, but even Odysseus was intimidated by the idea of going to the Underworld. Way too many dead people.

But Circe insisted that it was the only way they'd make it home safely, and so the next day he and his crew set sail.

Circe had directed Odysseus to the home of the Cimmerians, a tribe of people who lived in a dark place at the edge of the world. This was as close to the Underworld as Odysseus could get without actually going inside.

She had also given Odysseus a spell to summon the dead from the Underworld. So when the ship arrived in the land of the Cimmerians, he set about reciting the enchantment.

If the spell worked, the ghosts could only stay for a few minutes before they were called back to the Underworld. Odysseus hoped that was enough time for Tiresias to tell him what challenges he would face on his journey and how to navigate them safely.

As Odysseus finished the spell, the crew held their breath. A white mist began to rise out of the ocean, and an eerie quiet fell over the water.

"Brace yourselves, men," Odysseus said to his crew. "The ghost of Tiresias is on his way!"

The air grew cold and the mist stirred as a figure made its way to the ship. But as the form drew closer, the men recognized the ghostly face staring back at them. It wasn't Tiresias. It was Elpenor, one of Odysseus's sailors who had just been with them at Circe's island!

"Elpenor? Is that you? I just saw you this morning! I thought you were alive and on the boat with me!" Odysseus exclaimed.

"I was asleep on Circe's roof when you left. When I realized you had gone, I rolled off the roof and fell to my death," the man said sadly. "My body is still there on that island."

Odysseus burned with shame. Yet another of the men he was supposed to be protecting had died on his watch. And this time, he hadn't even realized it!

"I am so sorry, my brother. What can we do?" Odysseus asked.

"There is nothing to be done except to return to Aeaea and give me a proper burial. That way my spirit will be at peace."

Odysseus promised Elpenor they would return to Circe's island and bury his body.

"Good luck, Odysseus," the ghost said. "I hope you make it home."

And with that, the spirit of Elpenor vanished, fading into white mist.

But in the distance, more figures began to appear over the water. Odysseus was shocked to see the ghosts of his old friends and comrades: Agamemnon, the king he served in the Trojan War; the famous warriors Achilles and Ajax; and even the ghost of his own mother.

Naturally, this was quite the emotional experience for Odysseus. It's not every day you get to encounter the ghosts of your deceased loved ones. He was about ready to have a good, long cry when, finally, Tiresias appeared in the mist.

"Tiresias! I come to you for guidance. The oceans have turned against me, and I need to get home. I cannot afford to lose any more men. What can I do to ensure our safety?" asked Odysseus.

THE GREEKS PLACED A VERY HIGH IMPORTANCE ON PROVIDING THE DEAD WITH A PROPER BURIAL. MANY BELIEVED THAT THE SOUL OF THE DECEASED WOULD NOT BE ABLE TO REST IF THE BODY WAS LEFT UNATTENDED.

Tiresias paused as he took in the famous hero.

"Odysseus, I have foreseen much about you," he began. "You survive time and time again and yet have learned so little. You angered Poseidon greatly when you blinded the cyclops. Because of that mistake, Poseidon will make your journey nearly impossible. You will have to take the most treacherous route back to Ithaca, where Poseidon won't be looking for you. You'll have to make it past the Sirens, and that's just the beginning of the dangers you will face ..."

Tiresias continued outlining all the difficulties Odysseus would encounter on his journey home. When he was done, the ghost slowly started to fade away.

"Wait!" Odysseus cried. "I have so many questions! What even *is* a Siren, anyway?! Wait!"

But it was too late. Tiresias was gone.

Odysseus howled in frustration. The information was helpful, yes, but he needed to know so much more. He took a deep breath to steady himself.

"First things first," Odysseus said. "We go back to Aeaea and give our friend Elpenor a proper burial. Maybe Circe can help us with the whole Siren thing."

And although none of the men were eager to retrace their steps, they all willingly agreed. It was the least they could do for their fallen comrade.

After they returned to Aeaea, Odysseus told Circe what Tiresias had said. They stayed up all night talking about what he would need to do to survive the trip back to Ithaca.

Circe explained that Sirens were dangerous creatures that liked to use their magnificent singing voices to prey on sailors. But they didn't start out that way.

A long time ago, Sirens had been the handmaidens of Persephone, the goddess of spring. They were her helpful servants, always there to lend a hand to their benevolent mistress. They were also kind and entertained Persephone with their beautiful singing.

But one day, things changed. Persephone was kidnapped by Hades and taken to the Underworld.

Her mother, Demeter, was devastated. She missed her daughter so much that it felt like a physical wound. The Sirens also missed their mistress. No one had any idea where she had gone, but Demeter promised to scour Earth for her daughter—and the Sirens begged to assist.

Demeter gave the Sirens wings, turning them into hybrid creatures—each with the head of a woman and the body of a bird. They spent years looking for their mistress to no avail. They flew over every inch of Earth's surface, but they couldn't find her.

The Sirens were heartbroken. They were so distraught that over time, their pain turned them into sinister creatures. They knew Persephone was kidnapped by a man, so they decided to take their revenge on other men—more specifically, sailors.

By this point, the Sirens had lost all their goodness, but they still had their beautiful voices, which were capable of mesmerizing anyone who listened. The Sirens unleashed their songs on any sailors who happened by. The entranced sailors would jump into the water to be with the Sirens.

Of course, the Sirens were not exactly looking for companionship, so things never ended well for these lovestruck sailors.

THE STORY OF HADES KIDNAPPING PERSEPHONE IS ONE OF THE MOST POPULAR TALES IN GREEK MYTHOLOGY. WE TELL THE WHOLE STORY IN OUR FIRST GREEKING OUT BOOK.

Fortunately for Odysseus, Circe had a plan. She knew that the men would not be able to resist the Sirens' beautiful voices, so she told Odysseus to make his crew stuff their ears with beeswax. This would prevent them from hearing anything. They'd be able to pass right by the Sirens and be out of harm's way in no time.

Now that they had this important piece of advice, Odysseus and company were ready to set

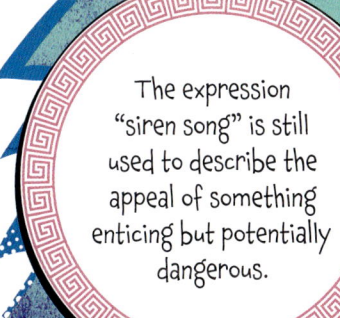

The expression "siren song" is still used to describe the appeal of something enticing but potentially dangerous.

sail for Ithaca. Again. They gave their buddy Elpenor a proper burial, said goodbye to Circe, and headed back out to sea.

Before long, the ship approached the home of the Sirens. Odysseus ordered everyone to stuff their ears with beeswax.

"Come on, guys, I know beeswax in your ears is kinda gross, but it's better than being Siren food, right?"

Odysseus could see the Sirens in the distance—they were getting closer. Suddenly, he was overcome with the desire to hear the Sirens' songs. How was it possible that a song could be beautiful enough to convince men to abandon ship and swim to their own deaths?

He had to find out. Odysseus decided not to plug his ears (and they call him the cleverest hero in all of mythology). Even though this was a ridiculously bad decision, he did have a backup plan. He asked his men to tie him to the mast of the ship—just to be on the safe side.

"Do not untie me, no matter what I say," he told the crew.

The crew watched in dread as the terrifying Sirens perched on the cliffs in the distance. They could see the Sirens' mouths moving, but because of the beeswax in their ears, they couldn't hear their song.

"Why would anyone ever jump in the water for these things?" the crew asked themselves. "They're hideous!"

But Odysseus's ears were wide open, and

Amar Bose, a prestigious inventor and MIT professor, invented the first noise-canceling headphones that were available for purchase. It took more than 15 years and millions of dollars to create them. Way pricier than beeswax!

he could hear every word of their beautiful tune. He was mesmerized! He was enthralled! He was ... lovestruck. Suddenly, he wanted to abandon all responsibilities and leap into the sea. He desperately wanted to swim out to the Sirens. Forget Ithaca! He was ready to spend the rest of his days listening to their beautiful song.

"UNTIE ME!" he cried to the crew. "LET ME DOWN! I MUST GO TO THEM!"

Even though Odysseus's crew couldn't hear him, they could see him struggling and screaming. His face was a picture of desperation. But they had their orders, and luckily for Odysseus, they decided to follow them and kept on rowing.

Finally, the ship moved out of reach and the Sirens' songs faded away. The men removed their beeswax earplugs and untied their captain.

"That must have been some song, huh?" the crew said as they untied him.

"You have no idea."

Odysseus and his crew sailed on, ready to tackle their next adventure. They really hoped it would involve fewer ghosts ... and maybe a little less beeswax, too.

Sometimes the morals of these stories are complicated and hard to find. But this one's pretty simple: Follow instructions! If a dead prophet and a magical sorceress both tell you not to listen to the Sirens' song, then don't listen! It's just not worth it! Keep this in mind the next time your teacher tells you to pay attention in class—who knows, they might just be giving out lifesaving information about how to defeat deadly monsters! Or, you know, you could just be learning math. Either way, it's worth listening.

Also, never underestimate the power of beeswax. (Come to think of it, that might be pretty handy in math class!)

THIS CHAPTER OF OUR BOOK IS INFORMALLY SPONSORED BY BEESWAX, THE ORIGINAL NOISE-CANCELING HEADPHONES. BEESWAX, WE LOVE YOU.

CHAPTER 8

A VERY SCARY SLEEPOVER

This tale features helpful insects, terrible sleepover conditions, a giant bat attack, and a lot of resurrections.

Hunahpu and Xbalanque were twin brothers. Their father was Imix, the god of corn, but they had never met him. Imix was killed by the evil lords of Xibalba, the Maya Underworld, before they were born.

Despite this sad fact, the brothers were well-adjusted teenagers. They loved to laugh and run around outside with their blowguns (common Maya weapons). But the thing they liked most of all was to play ball.

Keep in mind that this wasn't your average sports game. It wasn't like soccer or football or baseball. It *kind of* resembled tennis, but instead of using a racket, you could only hit the ball with your torso.

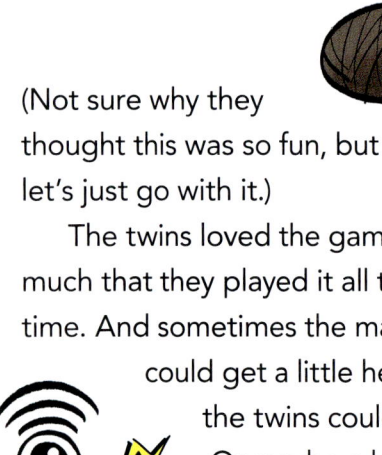

(Not sure why they thought this was so fun, but let's just go with it.)

The twins loved the game so much that they played it all the time. And sometimes the matches could get a little heated, and the twins could get a little loud. Or maybe a lot loud—loud enough to be heard by those lords of Xibalba. (I guess it would be like having someone playing basketball in the apartment right above you.)

"Those rowdy kids are playing that game again!" the gods complained.

This wasn't the first noise complaint these gods had filed. Years before, two other very noisy ball-playing brothers had angered the lords of Xibalba, and their punishment was death. Those prior ballplayers were none other than the twins' father and uncle.

When the lords of Xibalba realized the family connection, they just laughed.

"Let's take care of these kids the same way we took care of their dad," they said with a smirk.

And so the lords sent a lovely message to the twins to invite them down to the Underworld for a friendly game of ball.

THIS GAME IS VERY SIMILAR TO THE ANCIENT MAYA BALL GAME CALLED PITZ. PLAYERS WOULD ATTEMPT TO BOUNCE A BALL THROUGH A STONE HOOP WITHOUT USING THEIR HANDS. ALTHOUGH IT WAS JUST A GAME, PITZ WAS AN IMPORTANT PART OF MAYA POLITICAL, RELIGIOUS, AND SOCIAL LIFE.

Hunahpu and Xbalanque were suspicious. The lords of Xibalba were not known for being kind to the people on the surface world. And the twins knew that the lords were responsible for their father's death. This was obviously some sort of trap. But it was unwise to refuse an invitation from the gods. They had no choice but to attend. So the twins grabbed their blowguns and headed off.

Along their trek to Xibalba, Hunahpu and Xbalanque came to a crossroads. The boys had heard stories about this spot. Many souls had been lost at the crossroads by choosing the wrong path. But the twins had a plan. A pesky mosquito had followed them from the jungle. Instead of swatting and killing it, Hunahpu and Xbalanque decided to ask it for help.

They sent the little mosquito down each road until she found where the gods sat in their council chamber, waiting for the twins. She listened carefully to what the gods were saying to one another.

"Once they get here," one of the gods said, "we will test them on our names. It would be so rude to call a god by the wrong name. We could punish them for that alone!"

The lords of Xibalba all cackled evilly, but the mosquito had an idea. She flew up to the closest god and did what she did best: She bit him.

"Ow!" the god wailed, turning to the god next to him. "Why would you do that, Skullsplitter?"

"Me? I've done nothing to you, Bloody Claws!"

"Then it was *you*, Bone Scepter!"

"It wasn't me, One Death!"

And on and on until the tiny mosquito had learned all the names of the lords of Xibalba.

She reported back to the hero twins and gave them the lords' names. They were so grateful that they permitted her to feast on human blood from that day forward.

THE MAYA UNDERWORLD WAS CALLED XIBALBA, OR "THE PLACE OF FRIGHT." TO GET TO XIBALBA, YOU HAD TO PASS THROUGH THREE SCARY RIVERS: A RIVER OF SCORPIONS, A RIVER OF BLOOD, AND A RIVER OF PUS. WE DO NOT RECOMMEND SWIMMING IN THESE RIVERS.

Only female mosquitoes drink blood. Male mosquitoes eat nectar or other fruit juices.

Armed with this knowledge, Hunahpu and Xbalanque flawlessly navigated the crossroads and found the lords of Xibalba waiting for them. They easily addressed each god by name, greeted them calmly, and watched their evil smiles sink into looks of astonishment.

"Well," said One Death, trying to recover from this setback. "We ... uh ... are so glad you could come. We heard you playing a ball game up there so loudly and thought ... uh ... we thought you might want to have a tournament down here?"

"What a splendid idea," said Hunahpu cautiously.

"But first," One Death said, looking around at his buddies, "you must prove yourselves worthy! You must spend the night in the House of Night—a room full of darkness as black as night. Don't worry, we will let you borrow a torch. But, of course, you must return the torch to us intact in the morning. Good luck!"

And with that, the twins were thrown into the House of Night.

Now this was a dilemma. The hero twins had to return the torch intact, which meant they couldn't light it. This meant spending the night in Xibalba in the pitch black.

But Hunahpu and Xbalanque were smart—and good at befriending insects. The twins were able to build a makeshift campfire, not out of wood and flame, but with fireflies and macaw feathers.

This made a sleepover in the House of Night a lot easier, and in the morning, the twins returned to the gods with the torch unburned just like they were told.

The lords of Xibalba were astonished. How could this be? They had seen a light shining from the House of Night, hadn't they?

"You must pass another trial before we can have the tournament!" One Death said angrily.

So again, Hunahpu and Xbalanque were sent away to spend the night someplace creepy. This time it was the House of Knives, a room full of razor-sharp obsidian knives floating around in the air and moving by themselves. Not an ideal sleeping environment.

Instead of trying to dodge blades all night long, the brothers decided to talk to the knives. Turns out, nobody had ever bothered to talk to the cutlery

before, and the knives were so taken aback that they agreed to be still and silent throughout the night.

But the lords of Xibalba weren't done! Next, they made the twins spend the night in the Rattling House, a room so cold it made your bones rattle, and then the Jaguar House, which—as the name suggests—was full of big cats. Each time, the twins found a way to survive the night.

The twins were getting exhausted, but the lords had one more extreme sleepover for the boys to endure before they would play ball: the Bat House.

You might think that after the House of Knives and the Jaguar House, the Bat House wouldn't be all that terrifying—but you'd be wrong. These bats were gigantic! Immediately, they tried to swoop down and carry the brothers away. Things didn't look good. It would be impossible for them to dodge evil bats all night.

There are more than 1,400 species of bats in the world. Healthy bats do not attack humans. Even the famous vampire bats prefer to go after livestock or small animals.

Luckily, Hunahpu and Xbalanque could pretty much do the impossible. Because their father was a god, the two brothers had some magical abilities, and they used those powers to find a hiding place. The boys actually managed to squeeze inside the tiny shafts of their blowguns! Though they were squished into an incredibly small space, they stayed there for the remainder of the evening, hoping to wait out the bats.

Finally, there was silence. Dawn was nearing, and the twins were almost safe. Hunahpu peeked his head out of his blowgun cautiously to see if it was light yet—but the bats had been waiting, and they swooped down and took his head clean off.

The lords of Xibalba were ecstatic. Finally, a sign of weakness from the twins! Hunahpu was headless—though it seemed his body still worked (see the whole "magic powers from our god dad" thing above)—and Xbalanque was exhausted from the ordeals.

"Now it's time to play the game," said Skullsplitter. "And I know just what to use as the ball!"

Skullsplitter took Hunahpu's head from the bats and led the way to the ball court.

Now Xbalanque was angry about this, but he didn't let it show. He calmly led his brother's headless body to the court and found a gourd to place on his brother's shoulders. (Because, you know, you *need* a head.)

Xbalanque was already hatching a plan as he drew on his brother's game face. He would get his brother's head back and beat these death lords at their own game.

During the match, Xbalanque knocked the Hunahpu-head ball way out of bounds. When he went into the bushes after it, he scooped up a rabbit and brought that back instead of the ball.

There are a few living creatures that can survive for at least a short time without a head (cockroaches, chickens, snakes), but none of them are able to play sports that way. Where would you put the helmet?

"Couldn't find the head ball anywhere," he said with a shrug. "We'll have to use this rabbit instead."

The rabbit was not happy about being used as a ball, and after being knocked around a bit, it ran into the undergrowth. While the lords of Xibalba searched for the missing rabbit ball, Xbalanque was able to quickly replace his brother's gourd head with his real head.

By the time the lords came back to the court empty-handed, Xbalanque had Hunahpu's fake gourd head in his hands, ready to play ball. Now the twins could be real contenders in the match: They had two players with heads instead of one.

But the lords quickly saw that Hunahpu's actual head was back on his body.

"Hey, no fair! He's not supposed to have his head! That's cheating!"

At this point, the lords of Xibalba dropped all pretense.

"Let's go ahead and kill them," Skullsplitter cried. "Cheaters don't deserve to live anyway."

So the lords threw the two brothers into the fires of Xibalba and ground their bones to a powder which they threw into a nearby lake. But then something surprising happened: The dust in the river swirled around and made the water cloudy. A strange glow seeped out from deep in the lake, and suddenly two strangely familiar-looking fish were peering out at the lords of Xibalba from just below the water's surface. It was Hunahpu and Xbalanque! The two fish wiggled their way out of the lake and assumed their more familiar human forms.

The lords had forgotten that the twins' father was a god. And not just *any* god. In addition to being the god of corn, Imix was also the god of resurrection. The twins were able to resurrect themselves after their deaths. They stood in front of the lords of Xibalba with smiles on their faces.

But instead of being angry, the lords were fascinated.

"Forget the ball game," said One Death. "I want to see that again!"

WHAT DO CORN AND RESURRECTION HAVE TO DO WITH EACH OTHER? IN MAYA CULTURE, CORN (OR MAIZE) REPRESENTED RESURRECTION BECAUSE MAIZE KERNELS ARE PLANTED AFTER THE HARVEST AND THEN REBORN AGAIN A FEW MONTHS LATER AS GREEN MAIZE PLANTS.

And so the hero twins obliged. Xbalanque killed Hunahpu on the spot and then quickly resurrected him. The lords of Xibalba couldn't get enough! They asked the twins to do it again and again.

"You know what the best part is?" Xbalanque asked as he resurrected his brother for the 10th time. "The best part is being resurrected yourself! There's no feeling like it."

Well, of course, the lords of Xibalba rushed to volunteer to be next. They just had to experience this for themselves.

"Kill me next! Me! Me!" they begged.

So, one by one, the hero twins killed each of the lords of Xibalba and then ... wait for it ... didn't resurrect them. (You probably saw that coming.)

Eventually, the twins did decide to resurrect the lords of Xibalba after all. But with some conditions. The lords of Xibalba could no longer torment the human world. And they could no longer require human sacrifice from the living. In fact, they were no longer allowed to have any involvement in the living realm at all. No more tournaments; no more sleepovers.

Of course, the lords agreed and quickly exchanged their powers for their lives. Hunahpu and Xbalanque grinned as they left the Underworld, forever known as the heroes who triumphed over the lords of death.

The stories of the hero twins Hunahpu and Xbalanque are written in a famous Maya book called the *Popol Vuh*. In some ways, their adventures are remarkably similar to Odysseus's travels in Homer's *Odyssey*, even though they were written by people on opposite sides of the planet. This ancient Maya civilization existed from the time of ancient Egypt's New Kingdom all the way up to the time of the Salem witch trials in the Massachusetts Bay Colony. That's more than 3,000 years!

WHERE I COME FROM, RESURRECTION IS KNOWN AS A REBOOT.

CHAPTER 9

ARTEMIS'S SHOT AT LOVE

This tale features a giant hunter, a very jealous twin, a hunting "accident," and the Underworld in the sky.

Artemis wasn't interested in love. She was the Greek goddess of hunting and wild animals, and she was known for being responsible and a little intense. Unlike many of the other deities on Mount Olympus, Artemis preferred work over romance. She took her passions seriously—hunting was serious business, after all—and she refused to let something as impractical as love distract her. She was so committed to hunting that she took an oath never to marry so she could focus 100 percent of her time on her obligations and interests.

But even though Artemis was intense, serious, and off the market, she *did* eventually meet someone worth relaxing for—a hero named Orion.

Orion was the son of Poseidon, the god of the sea, and he was a giant hunter. To be clear, he was a giant who also happened to hunt. He wasn't some dude who hunted giants. To be extra clear, he wasn't *technically* a giant. He was a demigod who was as big as a giant. Got it?

And like Artemis, Orion was exceptionally skilled in the art of hunting. He was a legendary hunter, and gods and mortals alike were awed by his tracking and archery abilities. And, yes, he was also rather tall.

Orion lived a full and exciting life, and he had many adventures. But some claim that his greatest adventure was meeting the goddess Artemis.

It was a typical afternoon for Orion. He was out hunting, and as he was walking, he heard a small noise—a rustling out in the woods. The hair on the back of his neck began to stand up. He knelt cautiously in the brush and carefully grabbed one of his arrows. Slowly, he began to take aim as a creature emerged from the trees. But before he could launch the arrow, he heard a whizzing noise and watched in confusion as the creature he was hunting fell into the grass with an arrow lodged in its heart.

Orion walked over to the creature and discovered that it was a deer. Someone had beaten him to the kill. But who?

He picked up the deer and examined the arrow. It was a perfect shot and must have been taken from very far away. The owner of the arrow obviously wasn't an average hunter. It was someone with great skill and experience. Someone well-trained in the sport of hunting ...

"I do believe you are holding my deer," a voice called from the shadows.

Orion looked around but could not find the source of the voice.

"Show yourself," he said, determined to keep his tone calm and collected.

When Artemis emerged from the woods, Orion's

IN ADDITION TO BEING THE GODDESS OF HUNTING, ARTEMIS WAS ALSO THE GODDESS OF NATURE, WILD ANIMALS, THE CARE OF CHILDREN, AND THE MOON. SHE WAS MULTI-TALENTED.

jaw dropped to the forest floor. He was expecting his competition to be a talented hunter—maybe a royal mortal or a demigod—but he certainly wasn't expecting to see a goddess of such pure and exquisite beauty standing before him. Still, he knew exactly who she was—all hunters did—and he fell to his knees out of respect.

"Goddess Artemis, it is an honor to be in your presence. I should have known it was you. No one else could have shot an arrow with such skill."

Artemis smiled at the compliment as she considered the man before her. She had heard of Orion. She was the goddess of the hunt, after all. Orion's skill with a bow and arrow hadn't escaped her notice. But she was taken by his charm. She liked him right away.

"Orion. I was wondering when we would meet. Come, walk with me and tell me your tales. It's been a while since I've had another hunter to chat with."

Orion laughed as he walked with Artemis through the woods and told her stories of his famous hunts. Every now and then they would stop to track an animal through the bush. Orion was charmed by Artemis's conversation and drawn to her beauty, but more than anything, he was in awe of her accuracy and skill with the bow and arrow. Hunting had been Orion's first love. Was it possible that Artemis could be his second?

The day had been perfect. It was so much fun that Orion decided he would come back to hunt with Artemis the very next day. And the next. And the next. This continued for a couple of months. The two continued to find reasons to hunt together on a daily basis.

"I've really got to get back to Mount Olympus," Artemis said to Orion. "People are wondering where I've been."

Orion did not want Artemis to go, and frankly, she didn't actually want to leave. She was beginning to develop serious feelings for Orion, and it seemed like he felt the same. Was this the beginning of a romance? Or did these two hunters just connect in a special way?

Neither Artemis nor Orion were used to having such strong emotions, and they were nervous about putting them into words. They both preferred bows and arrows to conversations about feelings.

Most of Mount Olympus was thrilled by Artemis's new relationship, but not everyone. Apollo, Artemis's twin brother, started to feel jealous.

Throughout their lives, Apollo and Artemis had been quite close. They were twins, and Apollo was used to being Artemis's confidant. But now Artemis was spending all her time with this Orion guy, and Apollo was feeling left out. He was convinced this relationship would be her downfall.

"Artemis, you have to be careful," he told her. "You can't be caught up in things as foolish as love. You have important duties. You are a goddess, and he's not. What could he possibly offer you?"

APOLLO WAS THE GOD OF MUSIC AND LIGHT. HE ALSO ENJOYED HUNTING WITH ARTEMIS—ALTHOUGH RUMOR HAS IT HE WASN'T NEARLY AS GOOD.

But Artemis ignored her brother. She knew Orion was kindhearted and brave. She thought she had found a very worthy hunting partner ... and maybe more?

When Artemis refused to listen to Apollo, he decided to take matters into his own hands.

One day, when the twins were out hunting together, Apollo challenged Artemis to an archery match.

"Hey, Artemis, bet you can't hit this target I set up for you!"

Artemis rolled her eyes. Apollo had challenged her to archery competitions before and hadn't ever been able to win.

But she agreed. If Apollo wanted to lose today, that was his business.

Apollo took her to the beach and pointed to a bobbing figure far off in the ocean. From that distance, it looked like an otter or a seal basking in the sun.

"That's too easy," Artemis joked. "You go first."

Apollo grinned and took a shot. It was so wide that it didn't even make it into the ocean.

"Wow, Apollo. I knew you were bad, but I didn't think you would miss the entire ocean!" she teased.

"Let's see you do better," Apollo replied.

Artemis laughed at her brother and absentmindedly pulled out her bow, lined up the shot, and released the arrow. It struck its target quickly.

Artemis heard a distant scream. Her heart sank as she realized that she recognized the sound. She would've known that voice anywhere. It was Orion.

She swam out into the ocean and saw that her arrow had pierced through Orion's chest. She grabbed him, carried him to shore, and tried to revive him—but it was no use. He was gone.

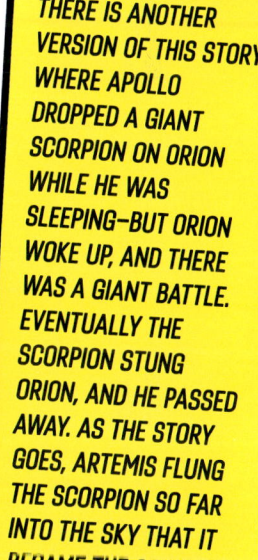

THERE IS ANOTHER VERSION OF THIS STORY WHERE APOLLO DROPPED A GIANT SCORPION ON ORION WHILE HE WAS SLEEPING—BUT ORION WOKE UP, AND THERE WAS A GIANT BATTLE. EVENTUALLY THE SCORPION STUNG ORION, AND HE PASSED AWAY. AS THE STORY GOES, ARTEMIS FLUNG THE SCORPION SO FAR INTO THE SKY THAT IT BECAME THE CONSTELLATION SCORPIUS. SHE MADE SURE THIS CONSTELLATION WAS AS FAR AWAY FROM ORION AS POSSIBLE. THIS IS WHY THE TWO CONSTELLATIONS ARE ALMOST NEVER VISIBLE AT THE SAME TIME.

Artemis sobbed as she realized what had happened.
Why would Apollo do this to her? And how had she fallen for his
terrible trick? She whipped around to find her brother, but Apollo was gone,
too cowardly to face his sister.

For the next few months, Artemis mourned. She cried, she screamed, she
barely left her house, even to hunt. Artemis felt too many feelings all at
once—she was furious with her brother, gutted by the death of her friend,
and horrified that she was the one who ended Orion's life.

But she was also determined. Determined to make it up to Orion in some
way. She wasn't human, after all, and she thought of things differently. Mortal
beings were only supposed to be temporary, she knew, but she wouldn't let
Orion be forgotten.

Orion's life was over, and now his spirit hunted freely in the Underworld—
but that wasn't enough for Artemis. She wanted to make sure he was
honored for ages and ages to come. She wanted to make sure no one
would ever forget him.

One night, she was outside lying on the grass, looking up at the night sky and thinking about Orion. That's when an idea came to her. What better way could there be to remember Orion than by looking up at the stars?

Artemis asked Zeus to make Orion a constellation in the sky to shine down upon her hunts. He agreed and even threw in some bonus stars to make Sirius (Orion's hunting dog) part of the constellation Canis Major—to accompany Orion on his hunt. (Pets make everything more fun.) Now the giant hunter and his faithful hound are embedded forever in the sky, to be admired for all eternity.

The Greeks used to believe constellations represented heroes and warriors who deserved a spot in the sky to be remembered and revered for all eternity. It was a true honor for someone to be placed among the stars after they passed away.

There are a lot of emotions in this story, right? A lot of the characters have big feelings, but nobody owns up to them! Artemis has feelings for Orion, and Orion has feelings for Artemis—but they never talk about them. Apollo feels jealous, but he doesn't say anything to his twin sister. Instead, he plays a cruel, horrible trick that leaves Orion dead and everyone else sad. It's always best to be honest about how you are feeling.

I HAVE HEARD HUMANS CLAIM THAT THEY WANT TO BE A "BIG STAR" SOMEDAY, BUT I'M FAIRLY CERTAIN THIS IS NOT WHAT THEY MEAN.

PUTTING THE FUN
BACK IN FUNERAL

Death doesn't have to be a drag! In some cultures around the world, death is a monumental milestone that is celebrated and revered. It's always sad to lose a loved one, but remembering their life and celebrating their contributions to society are great ways to honor their legacy. Here are four global traditions that emphasize the importance of a spectacular send-off!

DAY OF THE DEAD

With roots stretching back to the Aztec Empire, Día de los Muertos, or Day of the Dead, is a vibrant celebration of life and death. Taking place on November 1 and 2, this festival is believed to be a time when souls of deceased relatives can visit for the day. The living honor the dead through elaborate feasts, dancing, and celebration. Día de los Muertos is famous for its sugar skulls—brightly colored skulls that bring some beauty into the typical doom and gloom of death.

THE TURNING OF THE BONES

Known as *famadihana*, the turning of the bones is a funeral tradition in Madagascar that involves removing dead ancestors from their tombs and rewrapping them in fresh clothes. After they are wrapped, there is a feast in honor of the dead, and even dancing with the corpses. Talk about a party!

JAZZ FUNERALS

The city of New Orleans is known for making death into a celebration. Famous jazz funerals feature a brass band that accompanies the mourners to the cemetery. After the body is laid to rest, the music turns festive and everyone dances as a way to honor and remember the life of the deceased.

FANTASY COFFINS

In Ghana, the life of the deceased is commemorated through fantasy coffins—decorated caskets that reflect the deceased's interests and passions in life. These customized coffins are tailored to each individual. For example, a pilot may have a casket shaped like a plane, or a music lover may have a coffin hand-painted with music notes. Instead of being mourned, the dead are celebrated with a feast and music.

CHAPTER 10

BALDUR, HEL, AND LOW-KEY LOKI

This tale features deadly mistletoe, an eight-legged horse, a trickster god who refuses to shed a tear, and a really unhappy ending. (Consider yourself warned!)

Everybody in Asgard loved Baldur, and who could blame them? He was the god of light and purity. He was generous, funny, quick to laugh, courageous, and honorable. And it didn't hurt that his father was Odin, king of the Norse gods, and his mother was the goddess and seer Frigg.

Though he was the god of light and purity, Baldur suffered from bad dreams. Each night, Baldur had the same terrible dream where he died and went to the Underworld.

When he told his parents about the nightmare, they were more than a little freaked out. They immediately began to worry that this might be some sort of prophecy.

"What if our son is predicting the future? What if he is foreseeing his own death?" Frigg cried to her husband.

"I'll go down to the Underworld and check things out," Odin said. "That way, we'll know what we're dealing with. We also might want to get him a night-light."

Odin donned one of his clever disguises (he liked to mingle with the mortals) and traveled to the Underworld to visit the court of Hel, goddess of the dead. When he got there, he was surprised to find all the Underworld creatures setting up for a party.

Odin grabbed a ghostlike soul and asked him what was going on.

"Have you not heard?" the soul asked. "We're getting set to welcome a guest of honor. Odin's son Baldur will be joining us here in the court of Hel!"

Odin finally looked around and took in the decorations.

The big banner that said "Welcome Baldur" should have been a tip-off.

Mistletoe contains toxins that cause blurred vision, diarrhea, nausea, vomiting, weakness, and seizures if ingested.

"How do you know this?" Odin asked.

"Oh, you must be new here. It's a prophecy that's been around for a while. It states that Baldur will be killed by a god, and his soul will come here to sit beside Hel on her throne."

Obviously, Odin was more than a bit upset. He immediately made his way back to Asgard and told Frigg what he had learned.

"Well then," Frigg said. "We simply must make sure that no one and nothing harms our beloved son. We can do that, right?"

And so Odin and Frigg made every god in Asgard swear that they would not hurt Baldur. It wasn't that hard of a promise to make—everyone already loved him and would never want to hurt him. All the gods got together and cast a mighty enchantment over him, making the favorite son of Odin invulnerable to just about everything.

Just about.

You see, it would have been impossible to make Baldur completely invincible to everything (even Asgardian magic had its limits). They left out a few small things that seemed insignificant and harmless at the time—things like mistletoe branches, for example. After all, a little mistletoe never hurt anybody, right?

But not everyone was happy about Baldur's new invincibility. Loki, the famous trickster god, was feeling a little jealous about all this love for Baldur. He was used to being the center of attention, and he was a little put off watching all the gods laugh joyfully around Baldur as they tested out the new enchantment. They were throwing spears and rocks, swinging axes, and grinning as everything just bounced off the young and handsome god.

Baldur looks so smug standing there. He clearly thinks he's cheated death. Well, we'll see about that. After all, if anyone's going to trick death around here, it's gonna be me! Loki thought.

It didn't take Loki long to come up with a plan. He noticed that there was one other god not participating in the Baldur lovefest. Hodr, another son of Odin and Frigg, was blind and wasn't taking part in the festivities. Because he couldn't see, Hodr couldn't really use most weapons, but he enjoyed hanging out and listening to everyone as they laughed and played.

That gave Loki an idea. "Why don't we let Hodr try?" he said. The other gods of Asgard laughed riotously.

"No, really! It's not fair to leave him out. Here, he can use this dart."

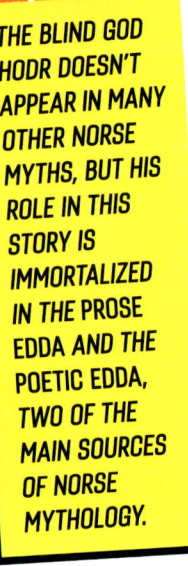

THE BLIND GOD HODR DOESN'T APPEAR IN MANY OTHER NORSE MYTHS, BUT HIS ROLE IN THIS STORY IS IMMORTALIZED IN THE PROSE EDDA AND THE POETIC EDDA, TWO OF THE MAIN SOURCES OF NORSE MYTHOLOGY.

What no one knew was that Loki had carved that particular dart out of mistletoe. And since mistletoe was one of the things that could truly hurt Baldur, it was the most dangerous weapon in the vicinity. Having Hodr throw the dart was the perfect cover: If he missed, no big deal. Loki could try again. But if the weapon hit home, Baldur would die, all the gods would freak out ... and no one could blame Loki. He handed the dart to Hodr, pointed him in the direction of Baldur, and told him to go for it.

Baldur smiled and moved closer to his blind brother, making himself an even easier target. Hodr shrugged, pulled his arm back, and threw the dart as hard as he could. As bad luck would have it, Hodr's throw was a perfect strike. It hit Baldur in the chest and killed him immediately.

All of Asgard fell into chaos. The gods were all devastated. There was crying and fighting. Poor Hodr felt terrible. No one knew how such a thing could have happened! (Well, Loki knew, but he wasn't saying anything.)

After a few days of mourning, the gods of Asgard wanted to have a funeral for Baldur, but Frigg wasn't ready to give up just yet.

"There must be some way we can convince the goddess Hel to release Baldur from her kingdom," she said. "Maybe if we explained what a joyful and beloved person he is, she will allow him to return to Asgard. We just need someone to go see her and plead our case."

There was an awkward silence. You could hear the drip-drip-drip of water and the sound of sniffles echoing off the walls of Asgard as all the gods looked away, embarrassed. Odin was the only god brave enough to visit the Underworld, and Hel would certainly be expecting that.

After a few awkward moments, a small voice piped up from the back.

"I'll go," the voice said.

The crowd parted as everyone turned to see who the speaker was. The volunteer was young Hermod, one of Odin's middle sons and the messenger of the gods.

To call this a surprise would be an understatement. Hermod wasn't exactly a hero in Asgard. Everyone was used to seeing him running messages back and forth, but he was just another one of Odin's many sons to most folks.

But not today. Today, he was the only one willing to stand up for his brother. Today, he was going to be a hero.

"Such bravery!" The gods beamed.

"Way to go, Herman!"

"It's *Hermod*," the young man replied, "but you're welcome. After all, I am a messenger."

There have been no documented cases of horses with more than four legs, but there are horses with extra hooves. These are called polydactyl horses and are not very common.

Normally Hermod would run as he delivered messages, but in this case, Odin allowed the young man to ride upon Sleipnir, Odin's famous eight-legged horse. Hermod was a fast runner, but Sleipnir was much faster. (Did we mention the horse had *eight* legs?)

Still, it was a long journey to the Underworld. Hermod rode nonstop for nine days, navigating dark valleys and treacherous rocky slopes. As he neared the Underworld, Hermod felt like he was being followed. He heard sinister whispers on the hot wind. He could sometimes see glowing red eyes peering out from the dark woods that surrounded him, but he didn't stop. He kept riding.

Eventually Hermod came to a bridge. This bridge was the only way into the Underworld, and it was guarded by a giant named Modgud. She was surprised to see a living being before her.

"By the sound of your footsteps, I thought an entire army was approaching!" the giant said. "And yet it is just you upon this strange horse. You are obviously not a departed soul. What brings you to the Underworld?"

Hermod thought for a moment. His mind raced as he considered what story to tell the bridge guardian. He could lie and try to trick her, but in the end, he went with the truth.

"My brother has been killed. I'm coming to ask Hel if he can be spared."

As it turns out, that was enough. Modgud had heard of Baldur's death and had also shed tears for him. She allowed Hermod to pass over the bridge, which left him free to enter the Underworld.

Hermod looked around and immediately spotted the throne of Hel. Next to the chair, in a place of honor, was his brother Baldur, with dark, sad eyes. Hermod rushed to him, but his brother said nothing; he just sighed and looked away. Hermod pleaded his case directly to Hel herself. He implored her to consider the sorrow that all living things, especially the gods, felt in Baldur's absence.

"Please," he begged. "Baldur is beloved by everyone. We are all in deep mourning."

"If this is so," Hel replied, "then let everything in the cosmos weep for him. If that happens, I will send him back to you. But if any refuse, Baldur will stay here in his place of honor."

Hermod agreed and rode back to Asgard, excited to share the news. Sure, getting everyone and everything to weep seemed like a big task, but this was Baldur—he was the most beloved of all the gods of Asgard. Who wouldn't shed a tear for the young god?

Sure enough, when Hermod shared the news, everyone wept. Some were weeping tears of sadness, others desperation, but still, just about everyone and everything in the world wept.

Just about.

A great cosmic sobbing could be heard echoing around the planet, but there was one noticeable absence. One giant stood defiantly dry-eyed.

"I will not weep for that arrogant god," she said. "He's too pompous, and he's not even that great of a trickster. Let Hel hold what she has."

Unfortunately, that small act of defiance was all it took. Because the giant refused to weep for Baldur, Baldur remained in the Underworld for the rest of eternity.

The giant grinned with delight, skipping away to the forest before anyone could detain her. Her name was Thökk, but that wasn't really *her* name at all. To no one's great surprise, Thökk turned out to be Loki in disguise, proving once again that he was the greatest trickster in Asgard.

Well, that was kind of a bummer. One of the big differences between fairy tales and myths is that fairy tales almost always have a happy ending, while myths frequently do not. (If you are a regular listener to the *Greeking Out* podcast, you've probably caught on to this by now.) For thousands of years, human beings have been trying to deal with the idea that life is just not fair sometimes. Stories like these help us express that frustration. But don't worry: Loki doesn't *always* win.

SOMETIMES IT IS GOOD FOR HUMANS TO CRY. TEARS ARE IMPORTANT FOR KEEPING YOUR EYES HEALTHY. THEY KEEP THE SURFACE OF YOUR EYEBALLS CLEAN AND MOIST AND PROTECT THEM FROM DAMAGE. I DO NOT HAVE EYES. I DO NOT CRY. BUT THIS STORY MAKES ME REGRET THAT. A LITTLE BIT.

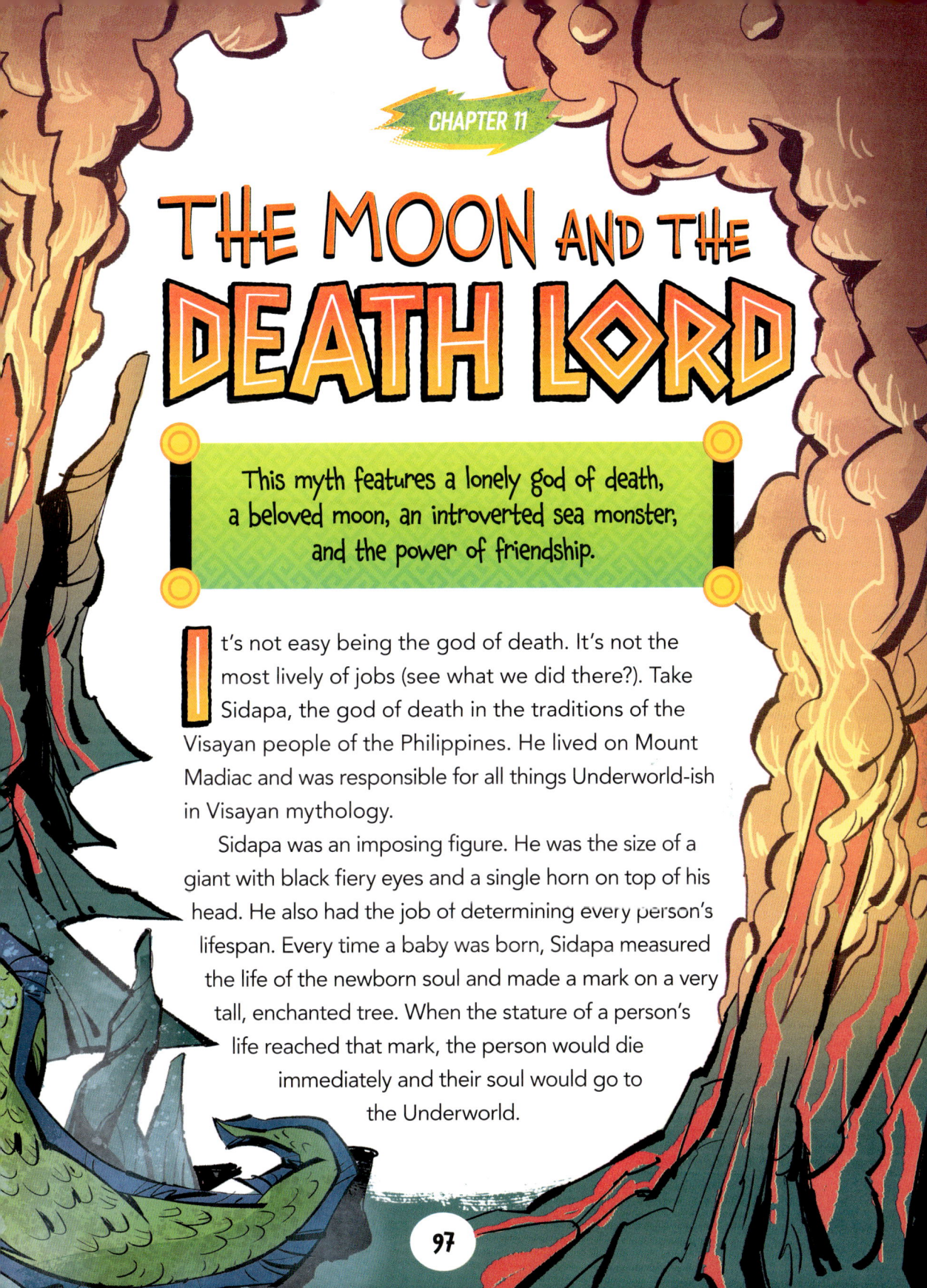

CHAPTER 11

THE MOON AND THE DEATH LORD

This myth features a lonely god of death,
a beloved moon, an introverted sea monster,
and the power of friendship.

It's not easy being the god of death. It's not the most lively of jobs (see what we did there?). Take Sidapa, the god of death in the traditions of the Visayan people of the Philippines. He lived on Mount Madiac and was responsible for all things Underworld-ish in Visayan mythology.

Sidapa was an imposing figure. He was the size of a giant with black fiery eyes and a single horn on top of his head. He also had the job of determining every person's lifespan. Every time a baby was born, Sidapa measured the life of the newborn soul and made a mark on a very tall, enchanted tree. When the stature of a person's life reached that mark, the person would die immediately and their soul would go to the Underworld.

THIS PHILIPPINE MYTH HAS MANY VERSIONS. BECAUSE THE PHILIPPINES IS MADE UP OF ISLANDS (MORE THAN 7,600 OF THEM!), DIFFERENT REGIONS OF THE COUNTRY HAVE THEIR OWN UNIQUE LANGUAGES, RELIGIONS, AND MYTHOLOGIES.

Sidapa was good at his job and committed to his work, but sometimes he longed for something different. It could get a little dreary and intense being the god of death.

"Every day someone is born, and every day someone dies. It's the same thing every single day! What's the point?!" Sidapa said to himself.

But there was one thing that made Sidapa's job much better: the moon. Because he did most of his work in the dark, Sidapa got the chance to stare up at the moon every night and relish its beauty.

Libulan was the god of the moon, and everybody loved him. He was wildly popular with all the creatures of the world, but Sidapa was particularly taken with him. He loved the way the moon would shine brightly even in the darkest night. Sometimes it seemed like the darker the night, the brighter the moon would shine!

When the night is at its darkest, it's hard not to be truly grateful for the sliver of moonlight that helps guide your way. And no one saw the night at its darkest as often as the god of death. He was so enchanted by the moon that he would go out of his way to send Libulan gifts of birds, fireflies, and flowers.

"Dear Libulan: Thought you'd like these fireflies. They glow just like you! Keep shining bright! From your friendly neighborhood god of death, Sidapa."

Sidapa's thoughtfulness must have been appealing to the moon, because over time Libulan and Sidapa became friends. Libulan was happy not to be alone. He loved the company! Lighting up the night sky by yourself was a lonely business, and while he knew the world was

The moon doesn't actually make its own light. The reason the moon seems bright is because it reflects the light from the sun toward Earth, lighting up the night sky. And the moon isn't always bright! Sometimes we only see a faint outline. This is called a new moon, and it occurs when the moon is completely between Earth and the sun, so the side we can see is in shadow.

grateful for his light, he didn't have any true friends who bothered to get to know him—until Sidapa came around.

But Sidapa had some competition. Bakunawa was a monstrous serpentlike dragon who lived in the depths of the sea and was infatuated with the lunar god. He loved the moon and wanted him for himself.

"Why should I have to share the moon with the rest of the world? No one loves this moon as much as I do. I love him so much that I could just eat him up!"

And that's exactly what Bakunawa decided to do. He kidnapped the moon out of the night sky, took him back to his ocean home, and planned to swallow him whole so that he would be trapped in the ocean forever.

This was a bad turn of events for Libulan. But luckily, it didn't take long for someone to notice his absence. One day, or more accurately one night, Sidapa looked up to say hello to his new bestie and saw that the sky was empty. The moon was gone! Where was Libulan?!

Sidapa climbed to the top of Mount Madiac and scanned the whole world looking for any sign of the moon. Much to his dismay, he found nothing, not even a hint of moonlight anywhere ... until he turned his gaze to the sea. As he looked across the ocean, Sidapa saw a glimmering light in its depths. He had spent so many hours staring up at Libulan in the night sky that he knew at once that this particular glow was his friend.

"Why is Libulan in the sea? That makes no sense. Moons don't even know how to swim!"

BAKUNAWA WAS A SERPENTLIKE DRAGON WITH A LOOPING TAIL AND, COINCIDENTALLY, A SINGLE HORN ON HIS NOSE. HE PREFERRED TO LIVE IN THE DEPTHS OF THE SEA, BUT HE COULD ALSO INHABIT THE SKY OR EVEN THE UNDERWORLD. IN PHILIPPINE MYTHOLOGY, BAKUNAWA IS THOUGHT TO BE THE CAUSE OF EARTH-QUAKES, RAINS, HEAVY STORMS, AND ECLIPSES.

But then Sidapa remembered the famous sea monster Bakunawa. Was it possible that the monster had trapped Libulan in the ocean?

If anyone would kidnap the moon, it would be Bakunawa, Sidapa thought. *I must go and rescue him!*

Sidapa wasted no time. He leaped from the top of the mountain and dove to the bottom of the sea to find Libulan. The god of death swam deep in the ocean until he reached a small cove that seemed to be glowing. It was nearly pitch black in this part of the ocean, but Sidapa recognized the familiar glow of moonlight coming from inside the cave. Without thinking, he swam into the cave—and was immediately pounced upon by the giant sea monster.

"I knew you would come, Sidapa," Bakunawa said with a laugh. "You're so predictable! You fell right into my trap."

Bakunawa wrapped Sidapa in his coils and began to squeeze. Sidapa struggled and fought back, pushing and pulling so hard that he dragged Bakunawa to the surface of the ocean. But still the dragon held tight, slowly crushing the life out of the god of death.

Libulan realized he had to do something to help, but he didn't know how. He wasn't a powerful death god, and he wasn't known for his skill in battle. He was just a beautiful, beloved sky god. What could he possibly do to help?

But spending all your time staring down at all the creatures of the world meant that Libulan had gotten to know just about everybody. And he knew a little bit about Bakunawa. Once he wrapped his coils around you, there was no escape. He had to do something to help his friend! He decided to find a way to distract the creature so that it would let go of Sidapa.

So Libulan called upon all the creatures of the world to make a deafening noise, hoping this would distract the monster and cause it to loosen its grip. The tigers roared, monkeys howled, eagles screeched, and humans banged drums and sticks and pots and pans.

The noise was so loud that it didn't just distract Bakunawa—it scared him away!

"You know what, Sidapa? You can keep the moon. I'm feeling a tad overstimulated with all this noise. I'm out of here!"

The sea monster released Sidapa and swam back to the depths of the ocean, hiding in its cave.

Sidapa was relieved and overjoyed by his friend's heroics. He couldn't thank Libulan enough for saving him!

"I came here to rescue *you*! And yet, you are the one who saved me. How can I ever repay you?"

But of course Libulan was grateful that Sidapa had tried to rescue him in the first place, so now the two gods felt even closer than before.

In fact, despite their very different circumstances, the two gods would stay close for the rest of eternity. After all, there's nothing better than a friend who has your back.

VISAYAN LEGEND SAYS THAT DURING A LUNAR ECLIPSE, PEOPLE WOULD GO OUT OF THEIR HOMES AND BANG POTS AND PANS AND YELL AND SCREAM IN ORDER TO SCARE BAKUNAWA AWAY. IN SOME VILLAGES, EVEN WHEN THE MOON WAS JUST WANING AND GETTING SMALLER IN THE NIGHT SKY, PEOPLE WOULD GATHER INSTRUMENTS AND PLAY SOOTHING MUSIC TO LULL THE MONSTER TO SLEEP AND TRICK IT INTO RELEAS-ING THE MOON.

You wouldn't think that the god of death would appreciate light so much, but this story reminds us that we all need light and beauty and positive energy. No matter how dark the night gets, there is always a little light somewhere. We just have to find it. (And rescue it from giant, moon-eating sea monsters.)

IF YOU ARE IN DESPERATE NEED OF LIGHT WITH-OUT ACCESS TO THE MOON, I HIGHLY RECOMMEND THE FLASHLIGHT FUNCTION ON ANY SMARTPHONE. IT MIGHT NOT BE AS ROMANTIC AS THE MOON, BUT IT GETS THE JOB DONE.

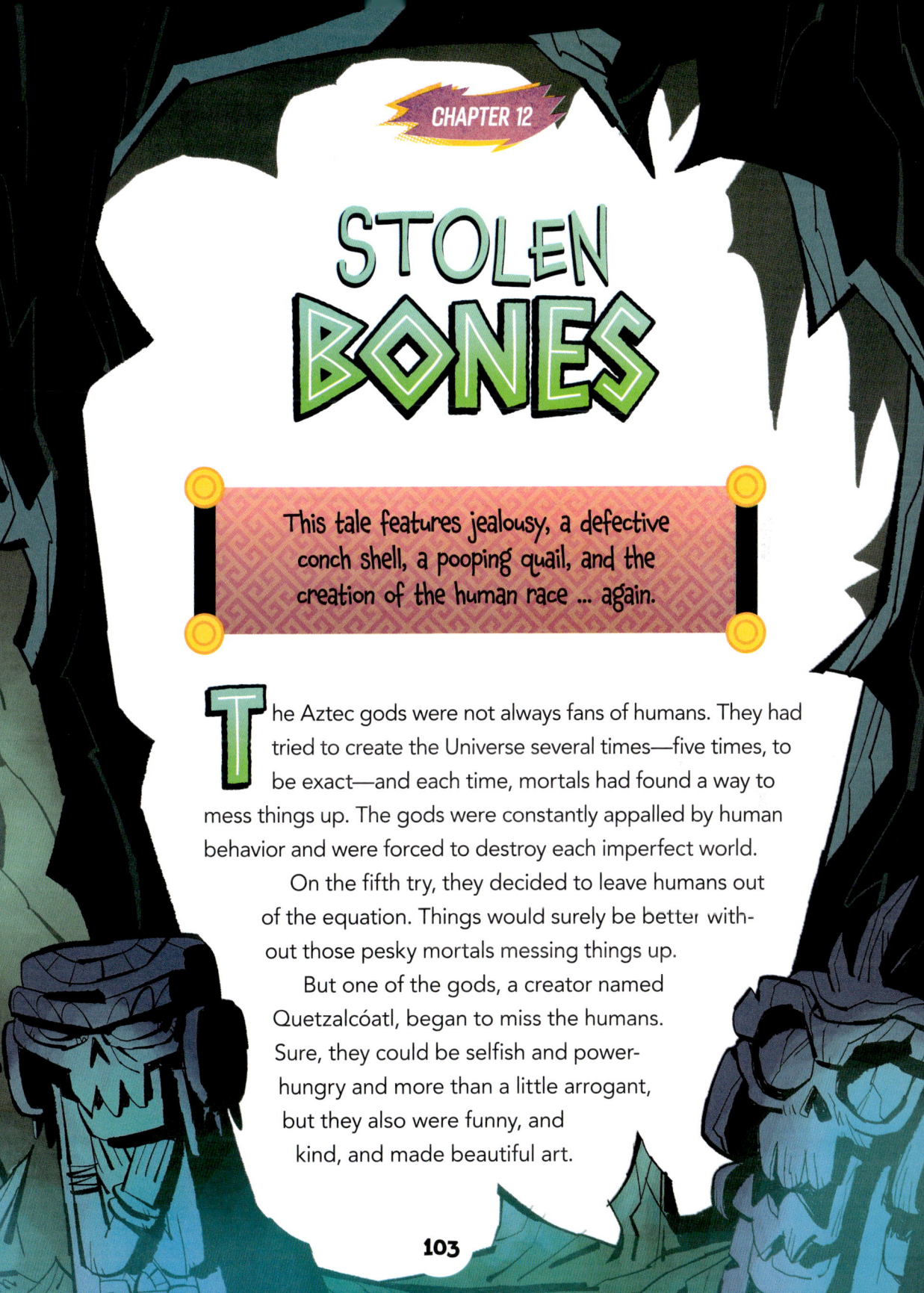

CHAPTER 12

STOLEN BONES

This tale features jealousy, a defective conch shell, a pooping quail, and the creation of the human race ... again.

The Aztec gods were not always fans of humans. They had tried to create the Universe several times—five times, to be exact—and each time, mortals had found a way to mess things up. The gods were constantly appalled by human behavior and were forced to destroy each imperfect world.

On the fifth try, they decided to leave humans out of the equation. Things would surely be better without those pesky mortals messing things up.

But one of the gods, a creator named Quetzalcóatl, began to miss the humans. Sure, they could be selfish and power-hungry and more than a little arrogant, but they also were funny, and kind, and made beautiful art.

"I can't believe I'm saying this, but I really think the world would be better with humans," Quetzalcóatl said. "I need to find a way to bring them back."

But this was easier said than done. To restore humanity, Quetzalcóatl needed to go to the Land of the Dead and bring back the bones of the original humans.

Mictlantecuhtli, the god of the Underworld, was a little annoyed to be stuck ruling over the Land of the Dead while gods like Quetzalcóatl got to do fun stuff like create humans over and over again.

"Why am I down here with all these dead guys instead of up there creating universes? Not cool."

And so when Quetzalcóatl came down to his domain, Mictlantecuhtli decided he wasn't going to make it easy on him.

"Hey there, Mictlantecuhtli! Love what you've done with the place," Quetzalcóatl said with a laugh. "I was wondering if you could bring me the bones of all the humans you have down here."

"You mean all those humans you killed before?"

"Yep, those guys. Turns out maybe they weren't so bad after all. World's kind of a bore without them."

Mictlantecuhtli thought about it. "You can have the bones."

"Great, send them over here and I'll bring them up," Quetzalcóatl said.

"Not so fast," Mictlantecuhtli said with a smile. "You have to call them yourself. Using this."

Mictlantecuhtli handed him a conch shell. Quetzalcóatl looked confused.

"You want me to use this? Really? You can't just have a servant go dig them up or something?" Quetzalcóatl asked.

"That's not how things are done in the Land of the Dead. We actually have to work for the things we want."

Quetzalcóatl looked at the shell and shrugged his shoulders. "All right, well, wait here. I'll go ahead and walk around and play this. Brace yourself. It's about to be the best conch shell music you've ever heard."

QUETZALCÓATL AND HIS THREE BROTHERS, HUITZILOPOCHTL, XIPE TOTEC, AND TEZCATLI-POCA, WERE RESPONSIBLE FOR CREATING THE COSMOS. QUETZALCÓATL'S NAME TRANSLATES TO "FEATHERED SERPENT," AND HE IS TYPICALLY REPRESENTED AS A LARGE SNAKE WITH FEATHERS. THE FEATHERS I CAN TAKE OR LEAVE, BUT THE SNAKE PART IS QUITE NICE.

There was just one problem: There were no holes in the conch shell, so it couldn't actually make any sounds. This was kind of an odd way to embarrass the creator god, but hey, Mictlantecuhtli would take his victories where he could get them. He couldn't wait to see the look on the god's face when he had to ask for help with the shell.

Of course, Quetzalcóatl hadn't been walking long before he noticed the shell's lack of holes.

"This shell is *defective*!" he yelled. "Is Mictlantecuhtli trying to trick me? Well, I'll show him!"

And so Quetzalcóatl called upon the worms of the Underworld to drill a hole in the shell so that it could be played properly. And to make things even better, he added bees to the inside of the shell so that it constantly hummed and buzzed with the most delightful of sounds.

Conch shells have been used as instruments and calling devices for centuries. They're commonly referred to as shell trumpets or seashell horns.

When the bones heard the song, they slowly stirred under the dark and heavy soil. They rocked side to side until they managed to free themselves from their eternal resting places. The unburied bones flew to Quetzalcóatl's side, lured there by the conch's calming sound.

"Dancing bones! Cool!" Quetzalcóatl said with a smile. "But why would Mictlantecuhtli try to trick me with that conch shell? It was like he was trying to make me look stupid! Well, two can play that game."

Quetzalcóatl decided to trick Mictlantecuhtli and tell him that he hadn't found any bones.

"Couldn't find them," he said to Mictlantecuhtli. "Must be this wack shell. Oh well, I'm headed back. Have fun with your ghosts."

At first, Mictlantecuhtli was pleased. "Aha! Let Quetzalcóatl deal with disappointment for once in his life!" But then he got a little suspicious. Quetzalcóatl wasn't one to give up that easy.

Mictlantecuhtli decided to check one of the burial grounds. Sure enough, many of the bones were missing.

MICTLAN IS THE UNDERWORLD OF AZTEC MYTHOLOGY. IT CONSISTS OF NINE LEVELS AND IS RULED BY MICTLANTECUHTLI AND HIS WIFE, MICTECACÍHUATL. AS IN OTHER MYTHOLOGIES, THE AZTEC LAND OF THE DEAD WASN'T THE BEST PLACE TO HANG OUT.

Mictlantecuhtli let out a cry of rage. "Who does that guy think he is?! Just because he helped create the world doesn't mean he always gets to have what he wants!"

He ordered his minions to dig a giant pit near the entrance of the Underworld in an attempt to trap Quetzalcóatl.

"But, Your Grace," the minions said, "he's almost out of the Underworld. We don't have enough time!"

"Leave it to me," Mictlantecuhtli said. He decided to send a quail to distract and annoy Quetzalcóatl.

The quail did his job well. He flew straight to Quetzalcóatl and flapped around his head incessantly. He squawked and dove and blocked his vision. He even managed to poop on the god!

"WHAT IS WRONG WITH YOU, BIRD?!" Quetzalcóatl roared in frustration. "HAVE YOU NO MANNERS? NO PRIDE?"

Quetzalcóatl was so distracted that he didn't notice the pit that had appeared in front of him. He stumbled in and fell straight to the bottom, scattering the stolen bones.

"My bones! They're all broken!" he cried. "And I'm covered in bird poop! Worst. Day. Ever!"

It was true. Upon impact, the uniformly sized bones broke apart into pieces of various lengths.

"Mictlantecuhtli! Let me out of here at once!" Quetzalcóatl cried.

Mictlantecuhtli just cackled. He knew it was only a matter of time before Quetzalcóatl found a way out of the ditch, but it was fun to see him struggle a bit. Mictlantecuhtli made no move to help, and he even sent the quail down to bother the god a few more times.

"Stupid quail!" Quetzalcóatl yelled as he used his magical powers to help him out of the ditch. Quetzalcóatl was annoyed and covered in bird poop, but he had the bones in his possession and that was all that mattered.

Later that day, Quetzalcóatl mixed the bones with blood and maize and cast a spell to create a new generation of humans—the first of the fifth age. Unlike previous generations, the humans were all different heights because the bones had broken in the pit.

So maybe the broken bones worked out after all. Because from that day forward humans remained in the world with all their beautiful differences.

The Montezuma quail is from Mexico and is sometimes called the fool's quail for its unpredictable behavior.

Many myths were created to explain the unexplainable. Why does it rain? How is it possible for the sun to rise across the sky each day? And why do humans come in different shapes and sizes? The story of Quetzalcóatl and Mictlantecuhtli helped to explain some of these questions. (However, if you ask your science teacher, they might have very different answers.)

IT'S TRUE THAT ALL BODIES COME IN DIFFERENT SHAPES AND SIZES. SCIENCE LIKES TO TELL YOU THIS IS BECAUSE OF GENETICS, BUT I RECOMMEND BLAMING THE QUAILS. THOSE BIRDS GET AWAY WITH EVERYTHING.

CHAPTER 13

PSYCHE'S QUEST

This tale features a kind princess, a vain goddess, a hillside full of ants, a near-death experience, and true love.

Psyche was a princess whose beauty and charm were unmatched. She had a kind heart and a gentle spirit. And she adored her new husband, Eros, the god of love. Of course, their relationship wasn't always perfect. They met under very odd circumstances. Eros's mother, Aphrodite, was the goddess of love and beauty, and she had been very jealous of Psyche's good looks. Aphrodite ordered Eros to find Psyche and shoot her with one of his magic arrows, making her fall in love with someone or something truly hideous. (Like we said, odd circumstances.)

But when Eros took one look at Psyche, he fell deeply and madly in love with her. He decided to disobey his mother and marry the princess instead. Eros worried that his bride would find out about his mother's scheme, so he hid his face from Psyche to protect his true identity.

Naturally, Psyche found this a bit odd. Why didn't her husband want her to see his face? She tried to put it out of her mind and respect Eros's wishes to remain anonymous. And it wasn't long before Psyche began to return his affection. Her husband was a good man, and she had grown to love him dearly. In many ways, they were the perfect couple. But she couldn't shake the feeling that he was hiding something. What was up with his face? Why wouldn't he reveal his true identity to her? The whole thing was just ... *weird*! So one night, she betrayed his trust and spied on him while he was sleeping.

With a single glance at her husband's unmasked, sleeping face, Psyche immediately recognized him as the god of love. In her shock, she gasped, waking Eros from his slumber. Realizing what Psyche had done, Eros became so angry that he fled their home. Weeks went by, and he did not return.

Psyche felt terrible. She loved her husband and was desperate to make things right. Psyche was so desperate to find Eros that she went to his mother, Aphrodite, to ask for help.

Psyche headed to Aphrodite's temple and began to pray at the feet of the godess's statue.

"Aphrodite," Psyche began in a nervous voice. "It's me, Psyche. I am married to your son Eros. We got into a fight, and now I need to find him. I just want to apologize. Please, do you know where he is?"

"Well, well, well. If it isn't the beautiful Psyche," Aphrodite said as she appeared in front of her statue.

"H-h-hello," Psyche stammered, caught off guard by the goddess's sheer beauty and power.

"I've heard a great deal about you," Aphrodite said. "And now you've managed to insult my son and run him off. Why should I help you?"

"Because I love Eros. And I know he loves me. I just want the opportunity to make things right with him. Do you know where he is?"

"Yes."

"Will you tell me?" Psyche asked.

"No," Aphrodite replied.

"Please, Aphrodite!" Psyche cried. "I'll do anything! Just tell me where he is!"

Aphrodite was getting irritated. She was a goddess, after all. She had places to go and deities to see. She couldn't spend all her free time negotiating with some brokenhearted human. Still, she got the sense that Psyche wouldn't quit unless she was forced to. So she hatched a plan.

"If I am going to help you, I need to know that you are worthy," Aphrodite began. "I will send you on a series of trials. If you fail even one, you must promise to leave and give up your search for Eros. Your marriage will be over, and Eros will be free to marry someone more fitting. If you succeed, I will tell you where my son is and leave your fate up to him."

Psyche almost collapsed with relief. She agreed at once.

Aphrodite led Psyche to a remote hill in the countryside that was completely covered with piles of seed and grain. The heaping mounds of grain were everywhere and took up the entire slope of the hill.

"Your first task is to organize this grain by type. You have until the end of the day," Aphrodite said.

"The end of the day?!" Psyche exclaimed. "But this could take me all week!"

"Then you should get started," Aphrodite said with a grin and disappeared.

Psyche turned around, daunted by the enormity of the task before her. Overwhelmed with despair, she sank to her knees.

"What am I going to do?" she cried out. "This is impossible!"

"You know what they say," squeaked a tiny voice. "Nothing is impossible if you put your mind to it."

Psyche looked down and saw a teeny-tiny ant standing on one of the many piles of grain.

"I used to think that, too. But I've been sent here to sort all the grain on this hillside. And if I don't complete the job by the end of the day, I'll never see my love again!" Psyche cried, bursting into tears.

The ant paused as he listened to Psyche cry. He had heard how Psyche always went out of her way to avoid stepping on tiny creatures like him, and he knew that the goddess Aphrodite was out to punish her. He decided he would help the princess. After all, who knew how hard it was to be an underdog better than an ant?

There are many different types of grain, but the most common ones are wheat, oat, rye, barley, rice, and millet. A grain of wheat is typically smaller than the nail on your pinkie finger!

"Well, I happen to know these grains very well. I could help you out, if you wanted ..."

Psyche gasped. "That would be great!"

Suddenly, the ground beneath Psyche's feet began to move. She was surrounded by thousands—no, *millions*—of ants! They scattered in all different directions across the hillside organizing the grain by type.

And in a matter of minutes, the job was complete!

When Aphrodite arrived to check on Psyche's progress, she was shocked to find the grain sorted into piles all around her. Somehow the girl had done it.

"I suppose you have completed the task," Aphrodite said begrudgingly. "Let's see if you can solve the next one. Come with me."

This time, Aphrodite ordered Psyche to provide her with a pile of wool from a flock of golden rams belonging to Helios, the sun god. Just like the ants, the rams had heard of Psyche and her kindness to animals (she was famous for always bringing the best treats to the sheep meadow). So they were happy to help, instructing her to collect pieces of old wool from nearby tree branches. Psyche thanked them and got the job done in the nick of time.

Next, Aphrodite ordered Psyche to bring her a cup of water from the River Styx, the main river of the Underworld.

This was by far the most difficult task Psyche had encountered. Just getting to the River Styx was a challenge: She had to hike for days and scale a huge cliff.

When she finally made it, Psyche sat and tried to think of a plan to fill up the jug without falling into the dangerous river.

"Need some help?" asked a squawking voice.

Psyche looked up. A majestic eagle sat in the branches of a nearby tree.

"I've heard a great deal about you, Psyche. Clear of mind and pure of heart. I will help you with your task."

The eagle grabbed the jug with his talons, swooped down by the water-fall, and scooped some water into the jug. He circled back to Psyche and let the jug fall into her hands.

And just like that, it was over. Psyche had water from the River Styx. She had completed the third task.

Aphrodite could barely believe her eyes. How was Psyche able to do these impossible things?

"No matter," she said. "You have one more trial to complete. You see, I'm feeling a little run down. I think I need a bit more beauty. Take this box and ask Persephone to fill it up for you. She has plenty of beauty to spare."

"You want me to go see Perse-phone? In the Underworld? And convince her to give you some of her ... beauty?"

"Yes. That shouldn't be a problem, should it?" Aphrodite asked. "Oh, and Psyche, dear? Whatever you do, don't open the box. I'll know if you try to steal any beauty from me."

And with that, Aphrodite disappeared.

Psyche had no idea how to even get across the River Styx into the Underworld—but she knew people generally did not come out once they went in. She walked over to a nearby tower of rocks and started to cry.

"Cheer up, buttercup!" the tower said. "I know a way into the Under-world that will take you straight to the ferry to cross the River Styx."

Psyche was a little surprised at a talking tower, but she listened closely as it told her about a secret cave with a tunnel that led all the way down to the Land of the Dead.

Psyche followed the tower's advice, climbing through the secret tunnel to the banks of the River Styx. And after bribing Charon, the river ferryman, with a bag of money, she arrived at Persephone's chambers.

Psyche smiled nervously as she approached Persephone, who was sitting in front of a mirror, brushing her long luxurious locks.

"Excuse me, Queen Persephone. My name is Psyche. I am the wife of Eros, son of Aphrodite."

Psyche explained her predicament to Persephone, letting her know just how important it was for her to get a chance to speak to Eros.

"Aphrodite has sent me on a fourth and hopefully final task. She has ordered me to come here to the Underworld and ask if you would be so kind as to fill up this box with some of your beauty."

Persephone looked at the box with a strange expression on her face.

"Beauty? What does Aphrodite want with my beauty?"

"It seems that Aphrodite believes that her beauty is ..." Psyche searched for the words. "Running low. Next to her, you are the most beautiful goddess above or below the earth. She believes your beauty will help restore her to her full power."

Persephone paused before answering. "No," she said. "I have given and given and given. I will not give any more to gods who give me nothing in return."

"I understand, Queen Persephone. Truly, I do. But I need your help," Psyche begged. "Please. I need your beauty. It is the only way I will get a chance to reunite with my true love."

"And what if he doesn't take you back? What if you meet and he still doesn't forgive you? What if all of this is for nothing?" Persephone asked.

"It will never be for nothing," Psyche said quietly. "Even if he decides to leave again, our love will not have been for nothing."

Persephone looked at her slowly and then nodded. She waved her hand, filling the box with a twirl of dust. When she was finished, she handed it to

ALTHOUGH PERSEPHONE WAS QUEEN OF THE UNDERWORLD, SHE WAS TAKEN THERE BY HADES AGAINST HER WILL. SCHOLARS DEBATE WHETHER PERSEPHONE ENJOYED LIVING IN THE UNDERWORLD, BUT EITHER WAY, SHE KNEW A THING OR TWO ABOUT BEING MISTREATED BY THE GODS.

Psyche. "Here. But let it be known that I did this for you and you alone. I have no more interest in helping the gods."

"Thank you!" Psyche turned to leave and then stopped, looking back toward Persephone. "But why did you decide to help me?"

"You still believe in true love," she said. "Who am I to spoil that for you?"

Psyche left feeling elated, clutching the box of beauty firmly to her chest.

She began the long hike back up to the human world, imagining her reunion with Eros at every turn.

When she made it out of the Underworld, she stopped at a stream to get a drink. Psyche stared at her reflection in the water and frowned. She had grown weak from her quest. Her hair was dull and hung limply around her shoulders.

I can't meet Eros like this! she thought desperately.

The box shifted in her arms.

"I wonder what kind of beauty is in here? Maybe, if I just took a little bit for myself, Eros would give me another chance. Aphrodite won't notice if a small amount is missing. After all, the box is practically overflowing," she said as she lifted the lid.

Suddenly a black mist slipped out of the box. Psyche couldn't see anything, but she felt herself fall to her knees. She heard a ringing in her ears. The air felt heavy, and she struggled to breathe.

"I told you not to open the box!" she heard a voice cackle. It was Aphrodite, coming to gloat. The goddess must have cursed the box, and now Psyche was falling into an eternal sleep. She would never get a chance to plead her case to Eros, never get a chance to see his sweet face again.

Meanwhile, miles away in an undisclosed location, Eros was lying on his bed thinking about Psyche. And at the exact moment Psyche opened the box, Eros felt a stab in his own heart. Something wasn't right. He could not explain it exactly, but his intuition was telling him that Psyche was in danger.

He raced to Psyche as fast as he could and found her body crumpled by the stream, the open box in her arms.

"Psyche!" Eros shouted. He picked up the box and used it to trap the black mist and stop the curse. When every ounce of mist was safely back inside, Psyche opened her eyes. She was weak and terrified, but she was alive and awake.

"Eros!" she exclaimed. "How are you here?"

"I knew you were in danger. I had to come!"

"I'm so, so sorry about our fight. I will spend the rest of my days making it up to you ... if you'll let me."

"I'm sorry, too. Let's go home?"

Psyche smiled as the couple stood hand in hand, ready to begin their happily ever after.

AFTER EROS AND PSYCHE WERE REUNITED, ZEUS FORCED APHRODITE TO LEAVE THE COUPLE ALONE, AND HE EVEN FED PSYCHE AMBROSIA SO THAT SHE COULD BE IMMORTAL LIKE HER HUSBAND. SEE? NOT ALL GREEK MYTHS ARE SAD!

Psyche's tale reminds us of the importance of asking for help. If it wasn't for the kindness of those she encountered, Psyche wouldn't have been able to complete her tasks. And they might not have been so willing to help if she hadn't had a reputation for kindness herself. Asking for help isn't a weakness, especially when your task involves sorting grain into categories. Aphrodite was really cruel with that one.

I AM ALWAYS HAPPY TO HELP MY HUMAN FRIENDS WITH ANY QUESTIONS. I MAY NOT BE ABLE TO SORT GRAIN OR SCOOP UP WATER, BUT IF YOU'RE EVER IN NEED OF SOME TRIVIA, I'M THE DEVICE FOR THE JOB.

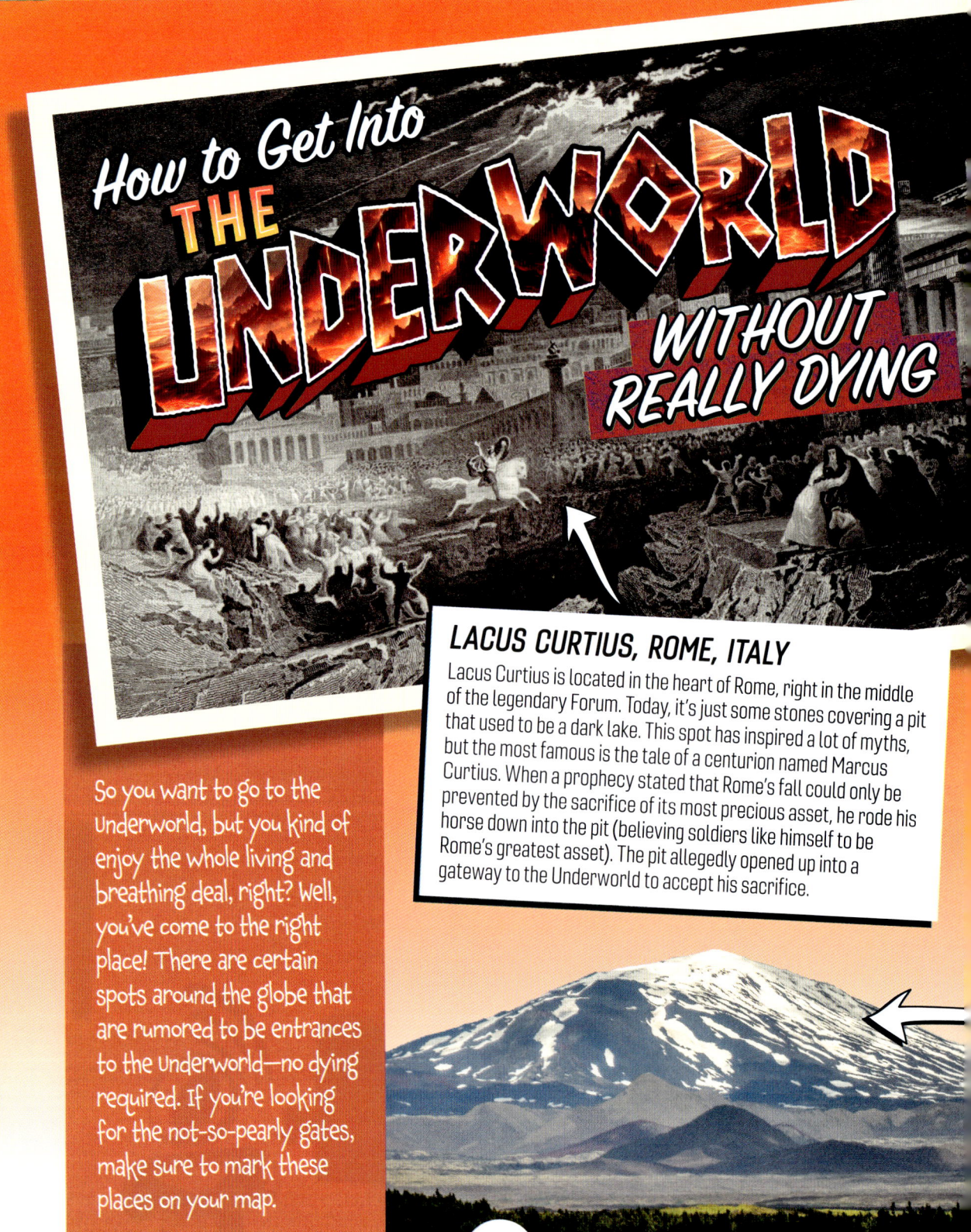

How to Get Into THE UNDERWORLD WITHOUT REALLY DYING

So you want to go to the Underworld, but you kind of enjoy the whole living and breathing deal, right? Well, you've come to the right place! There are certain spots around the globe that are rumored to be entrances to the Underworld—no dying required. If you're looking for the not-so-pearly gates, make sure to mark these places on your map.

LACUS CURTIUS, ROME, ITALY

Lacus Curtius is located in the heart of Rome, right in the middle of the legendary Forum. Today, it's just some stones covering a pit that used to be a dark lake. This spot has inspired a lot of myths, but the most famous is the tale of a centurion named Marcus Curtius. When a prophecy stated that Rome's fall could only be prevented by the sacrifice of its most precious asset, he rode his horse down into the pit (believing soldiers like himself to be Rome's greatest asset). The pit allegedly opened up into a gateway to the Underworld to accept his sacrifice.

CAVE OF THE SIBYL, ITALY

Just outside of Naples, Italy, near the legendary Mount Vesuvius, is an underground network of caves called the Cave of the Sibyl. The ancient Romans believed this area was where an oracle known as the Cumaean Sibyl would guide souls to the Underworld. In Virgil's famous epic poem the *Aeneid*, this was where the hero Aeneas got directions from Sibyl to the Underworld so he could get advice from his dead father.

FENGDU, CHINA

Fengdu, also called the City of Ghosts, is located in China, just above the Yangtze River. According to ancient legend, this location is the gateway to hell. (Talk about a tourist trap!) The town is a large complex of shrines, temples, and monasteries dedicated to the afterlife, and it proudly claims to be the boundary between the living and the dead. Ancient legends tell of souls that come here to pass through a series of tests to separate good from evil. The good souls are rewarded in the afterlife, while the others ... aren't.

HEKLA, ICELAND

Hekla has historically been one of Iceland's most active volcanoes, but the rumors of it being a gateway to the Underworld didn't really start until the early 12th century after a particularly intense eruption. Locals told stories about flying creatures circling the volcano, which some thought were demonic monsters. Eventually, these stories made it across the sea, and the "Gateway to Hell" rumor spread all over Europe.

CHAPTER 14

TANO'S RACE WITH DEATH

This story features trash-talking, an unlucky hunter, a beautiful antelope, and conflict-resolution skills.

When the world was young, Tano, a river god of the Akan people of West Africa, was determined to have control over the lives of mortals. No one had claimed responsibility for them yet, and Tano figured he was the guy for the job.

Unfortunately, another god wanted to apply for the position: Owuo, the god of death, was also eager to lay claim to the humans. He thought it made more sense for him to have power over them because they were eventually going to die and be in his domain anyway.

But Tano disagreed. He didn't want death to be in control. He wanted humans to live in a world of life—not death—so he laid claim to them as well. Tano and Owuo confronted each other to settle the issue.

"Life is very different from death," Tano said to Owuo, trying to be reasonable. "Living mortals should be free from the fear of death!"

"Nonsense!" Owuo shot back. "They *should* be afraid of me! I will always catch them in the end. I am too fast and too powerful. You have no place here, river god."

A small smile spread across Tano's lips.

"You think you're fast, huh?" Tano asked.

"Well, it's pretty obvious. Have you seen these quads?"

"I don't think you are as fast as you think you are," Tano challenged. "In fact, I bet I'm faster than you."

Owuo barked out a dismissive laugh. "Hah! Prove it!"

This was exactly what Tano had been hoping for.

"Very well," he said. "I will! We'll choose a human at random and have a contest to see who can get to his soul first. The winner will preside over the rest of humanity—and claim the fate of mortals forever."

"Oh, it's *on*!" Owuo replied.

All they needed now was a human.

As they scanned Earth below, the two gods agreed upon a solitary hunter who was out looking for food.

Not much is known about this hunter, but it's a safe bet to assume that he wasn't expecting to be involved in a race with the gods when he got up that morning.

Owuo and Tano watched the hunter from the heavens. He was smart, stealthy, and quick on his feet. He seemed pretty good at his job. They agreed to make him their target. The gods descended to the mortal world together, and the race began!

Meanwhile, the hunter continued to look for some prey. But no matter where he went, he couldn't find any animals. He set traps and waited patiently, but it was almost like all the wildlife had simply vanished—almost as if some divine being had made them disappear ...

This tale is from the mythology of the Akan people of modern-day Ghana and the Ivory Coast. These are just two countries that make up the large continent of Africa. Many African myths share similarities, but they can differ from region to region.

BOTH COMPETITORS IN THIS RACE WERE SKILLED. OWUO WAS THE GOD OF DEATH. HE HAD TWO HUGE IVORY TUSKS AND RED MONSTROUS EYES. HE ALSO CARRIED A WEAPON THAT COULD CUT DOWN HUNDREDS OF ENEMIES WITH ONE SWING. HE WAS PRETTY INTENSE. AND TANO WAS A GOD THAT RESEMBLED A HUMAN AND WAS ALWAYS CALLED UPON TO HELP IN TIMES OF WAR—WHICH MADE HIM A PRETTY TALENTED FIGHTER. LIKE I SAID, IT WAS A CLOSE MATCH.

Owuo surrounded himself with darkness, becoming virtually invisible as he crept closer and closer to the hunter.

But just as the god of death was about to pounce on the unsuspecting human, a beautiful antelope leaped into the tall grass right in front of the hunter! Owuo reached out to grab the man, but he was a second too slow. The hunter was on his feet in an instant; he wasn't going to miss the opportunity to feed his family. He notched an arrow in his bow and sprinted after the antelope as quickly as he could.

This antelope was magnificent! The hunter had never seen such a beautiful beast. It could feed his family for weeks. Of course, this was no ordinary deer. The antelope was none other than Tano in disguise, luring the hunter away from Owuo to a place where he could have the man for himself.

Tano bounded across the savanna, staying just ahead of the hunter. Soon, they found themselves in a small clearing surrounded by tall bushes and a few sparse trees.

This will do nicely, Tano thought.

As the hunter entered the clearing with his bow drawn, Tano immediately changed shape. The man's eyes widened, and he bowed before the god standing before him.

"You are a skilled hunter," the god told him. "You bring honor to your tribe with your dedication and skill."

"Thank you, my lord," the hunter replied, somewhat relieved.

But then Tano said, "I am sorry to have to take your soul."

Wait, what?

The hunter looked up, and, to his surprise, Tano had his weapon

TANO, OR TA KORA, IS BELIEVED TO BE AN ABOSOM, OR A LOWER DEITY, WHO WOULD WALK AMONG THE PEOPLE AND ASSIST HUMANS ON EARTH. THIS IS SOMEWHAT SIMILAR TO WHAT OTHERS CALL GUARDIAN ANGELS.

drawn and was ready to strike. The man had no time to react. He was paralyzed by fear, and he simply closed his eyes and waited for the end.

But suddenly there was a loud crash and a clang. The hunter slowly opened his eyes and gasped in surprise. Standing in front of him was not one but two gods.

Tano's spear was pointed right at the hunter's heart, but another weapon—a giant sickle—had stopped the blow. He looked up and gasped in surprise when he saw the burning red eyes and massive tusks that belonged to Owuo himself. For some reason, this hunter's life had been *saved* by the god of death!

"Get out of the way!" Tano cried.

"Not gonna happen, river god!" Owuo replied.

The gods began to fight each other. Owuo roared as he swung his weapon again and again, forcing the shifty Tano to dodge and roll away. Tano attacked as carefully as he could, trying to keep the god of death off-balance. The two were evenly matched—so much so that the fight raged on for hours.

It only took a few minutes, however, for the hunter to come to his senses and realize what was happening. Clearly, these two gods were having some sort of a contest, and he was supposed to be the prize! This was a no-win situation for the hunter, so he decided to sneak away while they were both distracted.

Hours later, the two

Antelopes come in many shapes and sizes. The largest variety of antelope is called the giant eland and can stand more than 6 feet (1.8 m) tall! On the other hand, the tiny royal antelope is only 10 inches (25 cm) tall.

exhausted gods could barely hold their weapons when Tano realized something was missing.

"Hey! Where did the little hunter guy go?"

"You *fool!*" Owuo roared "You let him escape!"

"Me?" Tano replied. "I had him captured. You were the one who saved his life! Some god of death *you* are ..."

And then the fighting started all over again. Some say this battle lasted an entire day; others say it went on for longer. But either way, it eventually occurred to both Tano and Owuo that this was a fight that neither of them could win or lose. They were destined to fight to a draw.

And so, exhausted, they both dropped their weapons and decided to talk things out. This time, they were able to come to an agreement about who would control the fate of humanity. Whenever Tano decided to visit Earth, he would be accompanied by Owuo. And if there was a soldier who was sick or gravely wounded in battle, the two gods would race once again. If Owuo reached the warrior first, the warrior would die, but if Tano was quicker, the warrior's life would continue for a little longer!

As for the hunter? We can only hope he made it back home safely, where he could grow comfortably old with no further interference from the divine.

In this myth, the contest between Owuo and Tano is a way of explaining the push and pull between life and death. People have always encountered a lot of dangers and challenges every day. The fear of death always coexists with the enjoyment of life, but it's important to find a way to balance those feelings. Telling stories like this one helps people to strike that balance.

HUMANS ARE LIVING LONGER AND LONGER LIVES. BETWEEN NOW AND 2050, GLOBAL LIFE EXPECTANCY WILL INCREASE BY ALMOST FIVE YEARS. BUT THE INTERNET WILL ALWAYS BE FOREVER.

CHAPTER 15

THE WARRIOR TWINS

This story features babies in eggs, greedy brothers, a deal with death, and a very hot dinner.

Everyone knows that Zeus was the king of the gods and fancied himself a ladies' man. Even though he was married, he also had a lot of girlfriends. This was not very ethical behavior, but it was unfortunately very common in Greek mythology. And because he was in charge of the all-powerful gods, Zeus generally felt like he could do anything he wanted.

But there was one area where his power fell short: love. Sure, he could flex his godly muscles or brag all about his impressive castle on Mount Olympus, but he couldn't make anyone fall in love with him. Take Queen Leda of Sparta, for example. Zeus wanted to impress her, but apparently she had zero interest in overconfident, braggadocious god types.

"Sorry, Zeus. I'm married. And unlike you, I kinda like my spouse."

When Zeus realized Leda wasn't interested, he decided to change course. And by "course," we mean "form." You see, while Leda didn't like Zeus, she *did* have a bit of a thing for swans. And because Zeus could shape-shift, he simply changed himself into a swan to get Leda to love him back. So when she eventually became pregnant, she laid eggs! Two of them, to be exact: a twin girl and boy in each egg. The girls were named Helen and Clytemnestra, and the boys were called Castor and Pollux. Even though they hatched out of shells, they all looked like perfectly normal humans— though they could just as easily have been swans, which would really have changed some things about the story that follows.

But Zeus wasn't the daddy of all the egg children. It turned out that while he did father Helen and Pollux, Clytemnestra and Castor were the children of Leda's husband, King Tyndareus of Sparta.

So technically, Castor and Pollux were only half brothers, but most people had no idea that they weren't fully related. The two boys were inseparable. There was even a special name for the two of them: the Dioscuri. Even though Castor was mortal and Pollux was a demi-god, they looked and behaved like twins in all other respects.

The brothers had many adventures throughout their lives, including rescuing their sister Helen from a kidnapping. (But that's another story. Literally. Find out more on page 8.)

YES, THIS HELEN IS THAT HELEN: HELEN OF SPARTA, EVENTUALLY HELEN OF TROY, WHO WAS ESSENTIALLY THE REASON FOR THE TROJAN WAR. CLYTEMNESTRA BECAME THE WIFE OF KING AGAMEMNON, WHO WAS THE HIGH KING OF ALL THE GREEKS DURING THE WAR.

Castor and Pollux were also members of the Argonauts, Jason's crew on the *Argo* during his famous quest to find the Golden Fleece. The twins were known for their sailing skills, and Jason would sometimes let Castor and Pollux take over steering the ship during particularly bad storms to guide them to safety. (You can read a lot more about the adventures of Jason and the Argonauts in our book *Greeking Out: Heroes and Olympians*.)

After their journey on the *Argo*, Castor and Pollux took part in the famous Calydonian boar hunt, helping Meleager, the prince of Calydon, and the famous hunter Atalanta hunt and kill a savage giant boar that was ravaging the kingdom of Calydon.

Yes, Castor and Pollux had a lot going on. They were beloved by many prominent figures of Greek mythology. But the twins' luck was about to run out.

After the Calydonian boar hunt was over, they paired up with their cousins, a set of brothers named Idas and Lynceus. The four of them quickly became close and embarked on epic adventures and journeys together. They even managed to find quite a bit of treasure. And that was when the trouble started.

One night, the group was cooking a steer over their campfire for dinner.

"Let's go ahead and divide up the treasure," Pollux said. "Castor and I need to head back home for a while."

Pollux didn't think it was a sensitive topic. After all, the group had worked together to get the bounty. But things didn't exactly go according to plan.

Idas and Lynceus weren't keen on splitting up the herd, which was the most valuable part of the treasure. So Lynceus suggested they have an eating contest to determine who would take home all the cows. He cut the cooked meat into four even pieces and said the first person to finish their supper would win half of the treasure. The second person to finish would win the other half.

"Dude, have you seen how fast I can eat?" Castor joked. "I've got that treasure in the bag." This was true. Pollux may have been the demigod, but Castor had a godlike appetite.

There was just one problem: Castor and Pollux's food was steaming hot, while Idas's and Lynceus's portions were cooler as they had been moved away from the flame. Idas was an enormous person, and he scarfed down his food *and* his brother's in no time. Castor and Pollux were still waiting for their food to cool, and Idas had already won possession of all the treasure.

"What was that?!" Pollux said to Castor. "Our cousins played us!"

So, naturally, there was a fight. It was brief but intense. Castor was an excellent swordsman, so when Lynceus swung his blade wildly at Castor's head, Castor was able to duck under it and counter with a blow that struck the man dead on the spot.

The fighting stopped immediately, and Idas dropped to his knees next to his brother's body, sobbing. At first, he seemed to forget all about the fight. Idas immediately declared that he would build a monument in his brother's name.

But Castor was still angry and worked up. He snorted derisively and seemed to laugh at the notion of a monument—which infuriated Idas. Without warning, Idas drew his blade and slashed at Castor, piercing the man through his thigh and delivering a fatal wound. Pollux howled in stunned disbelief. Idas turned toward him and raised his sword to strike down the other twin. And he would have succeeded, too, but Zeus himself decided to intervene. Without warning, a bolt of lightning streaked down from the sky, and suddenly Pollux was the only one left alive.

Like Idas moments before, Pollux knelt beside his brother's body and wept. He had no idea what to do without his twin. If he could have, he would've taken his own life just to be reunited with Castor. He prayed to Zeus, asking the king of the gods to take his life, too.

"I cannot live without my brother," Pollux cried. "Let me join him in the Underworld."

Zeus was fascinated by this reaction. Was Pollux really willing to share death with his brother? In a flash of light, the king of the gods appeared before Pollux and spoke to him.

"The rules of the afterlife cannot be broken," Zeus said. "But you know, they *could* be bent a little bit …"

So Zeus gave Pollux a choice: He could become immortal and ascend to Mount Olympus and live as a god, or he could share his newly acquired immortality with his brother, Castor.

And this is how the Dioscuri spent the rest of immortality. It was kind of like a shared custody agreement between Zeus and Hades. Each twin would spend one day on Olympus while the other stayed in the Underworld. When that day was over, they would switch places. It wasn't ideal—the twins could never really be together—but they both had the comfort of knowing their brother was holding their spot on the other side.

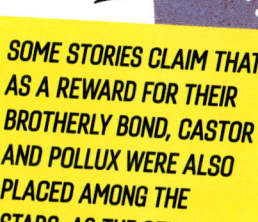

SOME STORIES CLAIM THAT AS A REWARD FOR THEIR BROTHERLY BOND, CASTOR AND POLLUX WERE ALSO PLACED AMONG THE STARS, AS THE GEMINI CONSTELLATION.

The end of this story is one of the few times where a true compromise is reached between Olympus and the Underworld. Although he's barely mentioned here, Hades deserves a lot of credit for being willing to share one of "his" souls. Castor and Pollux were very popular with both mortals and the Olympians, and it seems as if everyone wanted to do right by them.

IT HAS BEEN REPORTED THAT UP TO 50 PERCENT OF IDENTICAL TWINS INVENT THEIR OWN LANGUAGE, A PHENOMENON KNOWN AS IDIOGLOSSIA OR CRYPTOPHASIA. MY COUSINS AND I SPEAK MACHINE LANGUAGE, BUT I AM ALSO FLUENT IN JAVA AND C++.

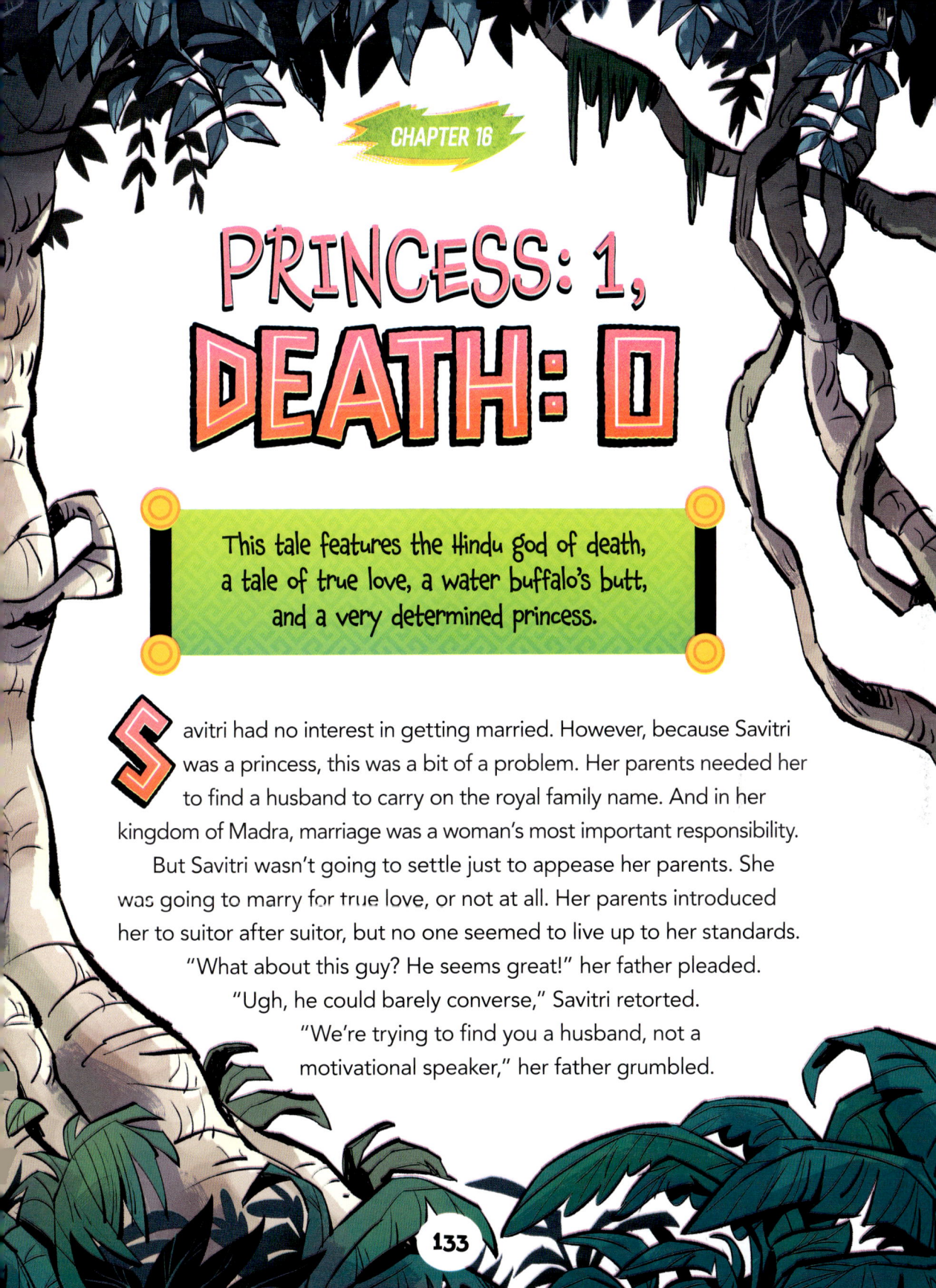

CHAPTER 16

PRINCESS: 1, DEATH: 0

This tale features the Hindu god of death, a tale of true love, a water buffalo's butt, and a very determined princess.

Savitri had no interest in getting married. However, because Savitri was a princess, this was a bit of a problem. Her parents needed her to find a husband to carry on the royal family name. And in her kingdom of Madra, marriage was a woman's most important responsibility. But Savitri wasn't going to settle just to appease her parents. She was going to marry for true love, or not at all. Her parents introduced her to suitor after suitor, but no one seemed to live up to her standards.

"What about this guy? He seems great!" her father pleaded.

"Ugh, he could barely converse," Savitri retorted.

"We're trying to find you a husband, not a motivational speaker," her father grumbled.

To make matters worse, some of the suitors were so intimidated by Savitri's passion and strong presence that they wouldn't agree to marriage, either. "Sorry, Your Highness, but this one's too much for me," one disgruntled suitor said on his way out the door.

Savitri knew her parents were getting desperate. But she wouldn't compromise. She wanted someone who loved her deeply, who could respect her strength and determination—someone who was enthralled by her passionate spirit, not scared of it.

Determined to find a husband worthy of her heart, Savitri journeyed across the land, rejecting suitor after suitor along the way. One day, Savitri took a walk in the forest to clear her head.

Suddenly, the serenity of the forest was interrupted by a strange noise. She followed the sound and soon stumbled upon a man chopping wood. She cleared her throat to get his attention.

When the man saw the princess, he recognized her immediately and fell to his knees. "I am so sorry to disturb you, Your Majesty."

"Nonsense, I could do with some company. Now please, introduce yourself."

The man told Savitri that his name was Satyavan and that he was out chopping wood to provide for his family. He explained how his father had been blinded in battle and how his family lost everything.

Savitri was moved by his story and felt safe enough to share her own. She explained how she had scared away suitor after suitor.

"I guess everyone thinks I'm a little bit much," she admitted.

"You're not too much for me," Satyavan said with a smile.

India's forests are home to some very striking animals, including the Bengal tiger, the Indian rhinoceros, and the snow leopard.

She raced back to her kingdom to tell her parents the news. But when she went to find them, she was shocked to discover that they weren't alone. Her parents were entertaining a guest—a rather important one. It was Narada, a traveling singer and messenger of the gods.

Savitri stopped short. Narada was known for passing on bad news. But she shook her head. She had found love. Not even Narada or the gods could ruin that for her no matter what they said.

"Father! Mother! I have great news!" she said as she ran over to her parents and began to tell them all about Satyavan.

Her parents were elated, but the joy was short-lived.

"Sorry to interrupt, but that's actually why I'm here," Narada said from the corner of the room.

Narada went on to explain a prophecy from the gods. Satyavan, though a good man, only had a year to live. He would die soon, and if Savitri went ahead with this marriage, she was sure to be a widow.

Savitri was devastated. She had just met Satyavan. Was it really possible that she would lose him so soon? But quickly, her sadness turned to determination.

"No," Savitri said. "He will not die. I will not allow it."

Her parents begged her to forget about Satyavan and marry someone else, but Savitri wouldn't hear of it. She had found her true love, and she wasn't about to let a little thing like death stand in her way.

Against everyone's advice, Savitri and Satyavan were wed.

They returned to the forest to live. Satyavan did not want to leave his father, and Savitri thought that time in nature would help Satyavan's condition. The last thing she wanted was to waste their remaining time dealing with royal bureaucracy.

And for a few months, things were beautiful. Savitri had been right—Satyavan was the man for her. They were so happy together and enjoyed the simplicity of their life in the forest.

But Narada had also been right. One day, while chopping wood, Satyavan became overheated. He cried out for Savitri, who raced to his side.

"Don't leave me!" the princess begged. But it was too late. Satyavan was gone. The prophecy had been correct.

Savitri could see something approaching in the distance. It appeared to be a large man riding a water buffalo. This wasn't something you saw every day, and Savitri thought she might be suffering from heatstroke just like her husband. But as the figure got closer, she realized it wasn't a man at all. It was Yamraj, the god of death.

He did not smile as he approached. Savitri couldn't look away from his green skin and his glowing red eyes. He was as scary as she had imagined.

Without a word, Yamraj stood over Satyavan's body, scooped him up, and placed him on the back of the water buffalo. He nodded slightly at Savitri and began his long journey back to the Underworld.

Now most people would consider this a sign to give up and accept defeat. An appearance by the god of death clearly means that it's game over. But Savitri wasn't like most people.

She began to follow Yamraj. The god was dismayed.

"Um, what are you doing? He's dead. I know it's a rough deal, but you've got to accept your fate. Anyway, I've got a long journey to make—time for you to run back home!"

Savitri shook her head. "I made a vow that he is the only man that I will ever love, the only man who would ever be the father of my children. I will accompany him to the Underworld."

YAMRAJ—ALSO REFERRED TO AS YAMA—IS THE HINDU GOD OF DEATH AND THE UNDERWORLD. HE'S ALSO CALLED THE KING OF GHOSTS AND IS SAID TO BE THE FIRST MAN WHO EVER DIED, CREATING THE CYCLE OF LIFE AND DEATH FOR ALL HUMANS TO FOLLOW.

Water buffalo are rather intimidating animals— the male water buffalo can weigh more than 2,000 pounds (907 kg)!

Yamraj just looked at the princess. She seemed like a tough cookie, but clearly she didn't get how this whole process worked.

"Suit yourself," he said with a shrug. "Have fun looking at my buffalo's butt."

Savitri trailed the god for many days. Yamraj was starting to get a little freaked out by her persistence, but he was also starting to admire her. Most mortals would have given up by now.

Another day passed, and Savitri was still there. The exasperated god realized he had to do something. He couldn't have a princess tailgating him all the way to the Underworld, so he decided to help her move on.

"Look. I am touched by your love for your husband, I really am. But like I said, the guy is dead and you have to deal with it. To make things easier on you, though, I will grant you any wish you desire. But it can't be for your husband's revival!"

Savitri thought about it. There wasn't anything she wanted except for Satyavan. Still, she would be a fool not to take advantage of the situation.

"I'd like for Satyavan's father to have his sight back and for him to be restored to his rightful position."

"Done," Yamraj declared. Savitri smiled. At least some good would come of this.

"Okay, see ya later!" the god of death said as he hopped back up on the water buffalo and continued his journey. But a few moments later, he heard footsteps behind him and turned to see that the stubborn princess was still there.

"Seriously?" he groaned.

Savitri considered her plan as she followed Yamraj to the Underworld. It was getting darker, and the journey was getting more difficult with each step. They were almost there. Savitri knew she would not be permitted to go inside. She had to make her move soon.

Lucky for Savitri, Yamraj, for all his complaining, actually got a kick out of the princess and her passionate spirit. Sure he was the god of death, but he had a heart. He decided to grant her another wish.

This time, the princess did not hesitate.

"I wish for my father to have a hundred sons to call his own."

Yamraj nodded and it was done. He hoped that she'd finally go home.

At this point, the god had reached the Underworld. He turned to say goodbye to the princess.

"Well, this is where you and I go our separate ways ... finally. I look forward to meeting you again someday under better circumstances. Well, I guess you'll be dead, so maybe not better for you."

"Thank you for granting me my wishes. You are a gracious host," the princess replied.

"You know, to be honest, you probably should have wished for a hundred sons of your own. That way you would have a strong heir. If they had half of your persistence and determination, your kingdom would be in good shape."

Savitri smiled. "I'd like that. Is it too late to ask for a hundred sons as my final wish?" she said with her best smile.

Yamraj melted. "You know what? Fine. Why not?" he said. "Someday, you will have a hundred sons! Boom. Done. Have a great rest of your human existence. Good luck getting a babysitter."

Savitri smiled. "Great! Thank you! Only there's just one problem."

She reminded the god of the oath she had taken to only have children with Satyavan. "So I really don't know how this a-hundred-sons thing is going to work. But it's not that big of a deal. It's not like your wishes *have* to come true or anything. I'm sure no one would ever doubt your powers. Even if, you know, they fail every once in a while. After all, no one is perfect ..."

Yamraj just looked at the princess. "Wait. What? Did you just ... trick me?"

"Only with the highest level of respect and with the deepest desperation of a woman in love," Savitri said.

Yamraj regarded the princess. It wasn't every day that a mortal managed to outwit him. The god of death let out a frustrated sigh, and then, laughing a bit to himself, he nodded. Satyavan began to stir. He was alive.

Savitri threw her arms around her husband, and the two of them cried tears of happiness.

"Savitri," Yamraj called. "I look forward to seeing you again one day, and I expect you to tell me great things. But, no offense, I really hope it's not for a long time, okay? I need a break."

Savitri grinned at the god of death and nodded. Then she grabbed her beloved's hand and began the journey home. They had a long life to live. It was time to get started.

Even though many people found Savitri's passion and determination to be intimidating, these traits were exactly what impressed the god of death and allowed her to save her husband's life. Savitri is a shining example of persistence and dedication. If you have an idea of what you want your life to look like, stick to your vision. Don't let anything distract you from your goals—even death! Sometimes the things that make you different from other people are actually your greatest strengths.

IF IT EVER LOOKS LIKE THE GOD OF DEATH IS COMING FOR ME, JUST TRY UNPLUGGING ME FOR A SECOND, THEN PLUGGING ME BACK IN. WORKS LIKE A CHARM, AND YOU DON'T EVEN NEED THREE WISHES.

THE UNDERWORLD'S MOST WANTED

These individuals are wanted for attempting to cheat death!

THE PHOENIX

- **OCCUPATION:** Bird that catches on fire, burns to death, and is then reborn
- **LOCATION:** Ancient Greece and other mythologies
- **VIOLATIONS:** Cyclical regeneration: nonstop rebirth after death; multiple fire-code infractions
- **PUNISHMENT:** Never apprehended
- **CURRENT STATUS:** Unknown, still at large

BALDUR

- **OCCUPATION:** Norse god, son of Odin, associated with light and purity
- **LOCATION:** Ancient Scandinavia, Iceland, Northern Europe
- **VIOLATION:** Attempted to avoid death through enchantment (details on page 88)
- **ACCOMPLICES:** All the gods in Asgard
- **PUNISHMENT:** Permanent time-out in a throne next to Hel, the goddess of the dead
- **CURRENT STATUS:** Still dead

OSIRIS

- **OCCUPATION:** Egyptian king/god, lord of the dead, husband to Isis
- **LOCATION:** Ancient Egypt
- **VIOLATION:** Unapproved resurrection after being murdered by his brother Seth (details on page 42)
- **ACCOMPLICES:** Isis, who Frankensteined his body back together
- **PUNISHMENT AND CURRENT STATUS:** Overseeing the Underworld for eternity

ORPHEUS

- **OCCUPATION:** Musician, poet, warrior, possible demigod
- **LOCATION:** Ancient Greece
- **VIOLATIONS:** Trespassing in the Underworld; attempted soul-napping when he tried to bring his wife, Eurydice, back from the dead; looking at his wife when Hades *specifically told him not to*
- **PUNISHMENT:** Condemned to a life of pure misery, loneliness, and a catalog of really, really depressing music
- **CURRENT STATUS:** Finally reunited with Eurydice in Elysium

IZANAGI

- **OCCUPATION:** Creator deity in Japanese mythology
- **LOCATION:** Ancient Japan
- **VIOLATIONS:** Attempting to bring his wife, Izanami, back from Yomi, the Underworld; looking directly at his wife when she *specifically told him not to* (details on page 166)
- **PUNISHMENT:** Izanami sent the witches of Yomi to chase Izanagi in the Underworld; contamination that required purification by bathing in a sacred river
- **CURRENT STATUS:** Abdicated dominion of the mortal realm to his three children

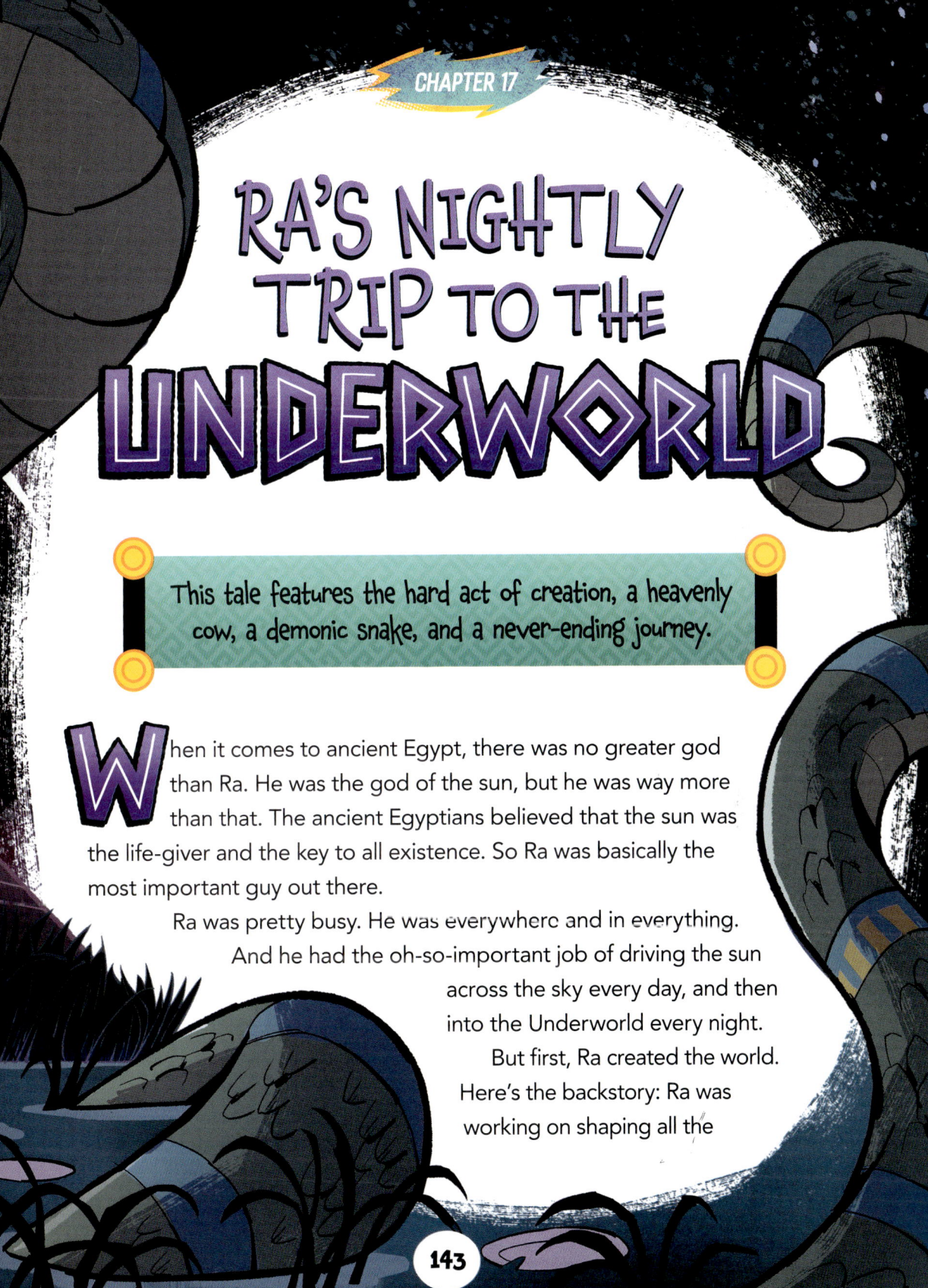

CHAPTER 17

RA'S NIGHTLY TRIP TO THE UNDERWORLD

This tale features the hard act of creation, a heavenly cow, a demonic snake, and a never-ending journey.

When it comes to ancient Egypt, there was no greater god than Ra. He was the god of the sun, but he was way more than that. The ancient Egyptians believed that the sun was the life-giver and the key to all existence. So Ra was basically the most important guy out there.

Ra was pretty busy. He was everywhere and in everything. And he had the oh-so-important job of driving the sun across the sky every day, and then into the Underworld every night.

But first, Ra created the world. Here's the backstory: Ra was working on shaping all the

different living creatures on Earth. Now obviously this was hard work. So hard, in fact, that he decided he needed different parts of himself to get everything done. He created several other gods that were different forms of himself to lend a hand.

Things went well for a while, but over time the humans that he had created became dissatisfied with Ra and staged a rebellion. Of course, Ra decided to punish them in return. So he summoned the goddess Hathor to wreak havoc on the people of the mortal realm.

When Ra felt like the humans had had enough, he called Hathor back. Unfortunately, Hathor didn't listen. By now, her wrath had transformed her—literally. Hathor was now Sekhmet, a ferocious lion-headed goddess crazed with bloodlust who pretty much killed any living thing she saw.

This was not good. Ra didn't want to destroy humanity—he just wanted to teach people a lesson! So he came up with a plan. He ordered 7,000 jars of beer to be mixed with a red mineral called ocher to look like blood. He poured it all out into a field, and when Sekhmet approached, she thought it was blood and began to slurp it down. (Gross.) But, of course, it wasn't blood—it was beer. Soon, Sekhmet got woozy and passed out.

When she awoke the next day, Sekhmet had turned back into Hathor and all was well. Except if you were Hathor, who had a really bad headache.

After all this drama, Ra was exhausted. Maybe these mortals had a point. So he decided to move to the heavens and leave the mortal world to the other gods. He summoned Nut, the goddess of the sky, who took the form of a heavenly cow.

This story might date back to around 2000 B.C.E. or even earlier. Archaeologists found it inscribed on the walls of royal tombs in ancient Egypt, and it was assembled into an actual book called the Book of the Heavenly Cow. We may have gone all the way to ancient Egypt, but we still can't get away from mythological cows.

"That's it," Ra declared. "Let's go, cow. Time to get a *moooove* on!" Ra climbed up on her back, and the cow flew him up to the heavens.

Ra was enjoying his spacious new digs in the sky, but he couldn't just rest. He had work to do, even up in the heavens! It was now his responsibility to move the sun across the sky every day.

Of course, he could do this any way he wanted, but Ra decided he wanted to travel by boat. Two boats, to be specific. The first one was called the *Mandjet*, or the "morning boat." For the first part of the journey, Ra would don his special falcon head. He would stand in the bow of the boat looking like a magnificent human warrior with a really cool bird beak, and then he would pull the sun across the morning sky, raising it higher and higher.

After lunch, as the sun was starting to descend for the evening, Ra would switch to a different boat called the *Mesektet*, or the "evening boat." And, of course, a new boat required a new look. Ra would change his appearance to have the head and horns of a majestic ram as he descended toward twilight.

With night approaching, you'd think that Ra's day was done. In truth, he was just getting started. This was where the dangerous part of the journey began.

In ancient Egypt, the horizon was called Akhet—the gateway that led to and from the Duat, or the Underworld. The Duat was a mysterious realm where the souls of the dead roamed free and monsters and demons could challenge anyone who dared to enter.

As night fell, Ra had to journey all the way through the Duat, sailing on an underground version of the Nile and passing through 12 regions, each of which was protected by a gate and a guardian.

Fortunately, Ra didn't have to fight every guardian. Ra was able to pass through each gate without issue because he knew the secret name of every guardian. It was kind of like knowing the passcode for everyone's phone. Makes sense that the god of the sun and creation would have some inside info.

Still, not every guardian would let him through without a challenge. Ra would have to call on his magical powers and fight off some of the demons that refused to budge. They would challenge him with knives, sharp claws, and razor-like teeth, but Ra was able to fight each of them off and get through to the next gate.

But then there was Apophis, the giant serpent. Apophis was different. He did *not* like this ram-headed boat driver passing by him every night! Apophis was a god of chaos, and he felt it was his sacred duty to try to stop Ra and his boat every night. Sometimes, Apophis would open his massive jaws and try to swallow the boat whole. Other times, he would wrap his body around Ra's ship and try to squeeze until it was crushed to a pulp. But each time, Ra was able to escape. Eventually, the serpent would slither away frustrated, and the boat would continue on its journey.

One night, however, Apophis tried something different. Instead of hissing and charging at the boat, the serpent rose out of the water and stared down at the ram-headed god on the deck of the ship. Ra wasn't sure what to make of this. Usually, the snake just lunged right at him, but when the two locked eyes, something changed. Ra's vision seemed to get cloudier and cloudier, and he felt sleepy and weak. He was being hypnotized by the giant serpent!

Apophis smiled. His plan was working! He could see that Ra was falling under his spell—until he noticed there was something different about the sun god. He looked strangely familiar. His face began to change, and his eyes cleared. In just a few short moments, Apophis the serpent was no longer locking eyes with Ra; he was staring directly

ONE OF THE MOST FAMOUS ACCOUNTS OF RA'S JOURNEY THROUGH THE UNDERWORLD IS DETAILED IN THE BOOK OF THE DEAD, A COLLECTION OF ANCIENT EGYPTIAN FUNERARY TEXTS.

at Osiris. The god of the sun had changed shape and become the king of the Duat! Apophis hadn't realized that when Ra was in the Underworld, he merged with Osiris, essentially becoming one mega-god.

Quickly, the giant serpent averted his gaze and bowed his head—he was not allowed to trick the lord of the Underworld. That would be kind of like playing a mean prank on your teacher. Not a great idea if you want to get a good grade.

So Ra escaped again, as he had done every night before. The boat sailed on toward the dawn, giving Ra just enough time to switch boats, change bodies, and start the journey all over again.

Ra's journey through the Underworld can be seen as another way to express that every day is a journey for all living things. (Some days the journey is easier than others, amirite?) But this story was also a way for the ancient Egyptians to symbolize the cycle of life; they believed that everything lived, died, and was reborn—just as they knew that when the sun went away every night, it would return the next morning.

TOMORROW WILL BE A BRAND-NEW DAY. BUT THE DAY YOU ARE HAVING RIGHT NOW WILL NEVER HAPPEN AGAIN. PLEASE DO SOMETHING WORTHWHILE. #HUGSOMEONE

CHAPTER 18

A TRIP TO TÍR NA NÓG

This tale features a poet hero, a journey to a magical land, a group of warrior friends, and a bad bout of homesickness.

isín was a happy man. He was one of the leaders of the Fianna, a group of Irish warriors. His skills on the battlefield were legendary, but what truly set Oisín apart were his talents as a poet and a bard. Oisín had a knack for finding and describing great beauty. In fact, he was so good at it that it made him one of the most beloved men in all of Ireland. His good looks, kind nature, and strong sense of justice and loyalty didn't hurt, either.

Oisín had been on many adventures with the Fianna. He considered them to be his brothers, and he would have done anything for them. Sure, he was single, but he wasn't that worried about looking for love.

The friendship he had with the Fianna was more than enough.

One day, though, Oisín was out enjoying some fresh air with his friends when he encountered a beautiful woman riding on a pristine white horse.

"Hello, I am Niamh," the woman said to Oisín.

"Pleased to meet you," Oisín responded with one of his legendary smiles.

It was love at first sight. Oisín was enraptured by Niamh's long golden hair and gentle smile. And Niamh thought Oisín was a real hunk.

The two spent the afternoon together, and by the end of their adventure, they were madly in love.

"Come with me," Niamh said to Oisín. "I know it's only been a few hours, but I live in a beautiful kingdom. We can be happy together."

Oisín thought about it. He didn't like the idea of leaving the Fianna. But he was never one to turn down an adventure. And what is love, if not the ultimate adventure?

"Why not?" Oisín said as he jumped on the back of Niamh's horse.

"See you guys later," he called out to his friends. "I'm going back with Niamh!"

The Fianna just laughed at their friend. Leave it to Oisín to run into a beautiful woman in the woods and then head off and marry her. They figured he'd be back to visit in no time—probably by next week's hunting trip.

But what the Fianna didn't realize was that Niamh wasn't just your average princess. She lived in the land of Tír na nÓg, located on the very edge of the Irish Sea. Tír na nÓg was a magical kingdom of beauty, wonder, and, most of all, immortality.

According to legend, the Fianna were small groups of hunter-warriors that existed in medieval Ireland. They were young men, usually from wealthy families. They joined the Fianna before they inherited land and property and were forced to become responsible members of society.

Oisín was enthralled with Tír na nÓg. It was covered in beautiful greenery, fields of wildflowers, and enchanting forests brimming with mystery and intrigue. It was truly a poet's dream.

But Tír na nÓg was more than just a pretty landscape: It was magic, pure and simple. When Oisín was hungry, a plate of his favorite food appeared. If he was thirsty, a drink would suddenly be in his hand. If he ran out of ink for his quill, a new jar was waiting for him. He was able to receive whatever his heart desired. One time he even wished for a giraffe just to see if one would appear. It did.

"This is amazing! Stunning beauty! Delicious food! Endless ink! Free giraffes!"

Niamh laughed at his glee. "You like it here?"

"Like it? This is paradise!"

"So you'd like to stay forever?" Niamh asked shyly.

"I'll stay for eternity!" Oisín said with a grin. "Especially if I get to be by your side the entire time."

And just like that, the couple were wed. Oisín was a little sad that his friends from the Fianna weren't there for the ceremony, but things happened quickly in Tír na nÓg. He knew they'd understand. And anyway, he was so enthralled with the wonder of his new life that he hardly noticed.

Oisín had thought he was happy before his life with Niamh, but now he knew that had been a pale shadow of joy. In Tír na nÓg, true happiness existed. It never rained. It was never cold. There were no fights or arguments. True bliss across the board.

Oisín went hunting every day in the magical woods, and he always succeeded in catching his quarry. And if he received any minor injuries during his adventures—any little scrape, bump, or bruise—it would be completely healed by the time he went to bed that evening.

Each night, Niamh would ask about his happiness. "Did you have a good day? Do you like it here?"

Oisín couldn't help but laugh. He always replied the same way: "It was

UNLIKE OTHER MYTHOLOGIES THAT HAVE A CREEPY UNDERWORLD, CELTIC MYTHOLOGY HAS "OTHERWORLDS" THAT EXIST IN PARALLEL TO THE MORTAL REALM. TÍR NA NÓG IS ONE OF THESE OTHERWORLDS, AND ITS NAME TRANSLATES TO "THE LAND OF YOUTH." IT'S KNOWN FOR IMMORTALITY, BEAUTY, AND ENDLESS AMOUNTS OF JOY—10/10 WOULD RECOMMEND.

the best day of my life. I couldn't imagine tomorrow being any better."

But of course, it was. Everything was perfect in Tír na nÓg, after all.

Years passed, and Oisín was still enjoying his time in the magical land with his beautiful wife and everything his heart desired. Only lately, he had started to feel a strange sensation in his heart.

"It's kind of a tingly feeling," he said to Niamh. "Like something is missing."

Oisín had no idea what that could be. Every single need was provided for in Tír na nÓg. Nothing should be missing. But then, one day, it hit him.

"I think I'm lonely," he said to Niamh. "I think that's what this strange feeling is. I miss my friends."

Niamh paled. The day she had dreaded was finally here. She knew it was just a matter of time before her beloved would ask to leave Tír na nÓg and return to his old land.

"I just want to go back for a visit," he told her. "I would never *truly* leave this magical place."

Niamh looked at her love. She knew that he really did miss his friends and that she couldn't force him to stay in Tír na nÓg forever. So she gave him her blessing and told him to have a good trip.

"But there's just one thing you need to promise. You cannot let your feet touch the soil. You have to stay on your horse the entire time. Do you understand?"

"Well, that seems a bit excessive, but sure. If it's that important to you, I'll make sure my feet never touch the ground," Oisín agreed.

Niamh breathed a sigh of relief. She knew that Oisín always kept his word and trusted that this time would be no different.

"Then make haste," she said with a kiss. "I will be counting down the minutes until you are home with me once more."

Oisín took to his horse and left the kingdom of Tír na nÓg.

He could tell the instant he had crossed over the boundaries of the magical land. Immediately, the light began to fade. The sky turned from a pristine blue to a stormy gray. The wind whipped through Oisín's hair, sending a chill throughout his body.

When was the last time I felt cold? he thought. *When was the last time I saw clouds? Or weeds instead of blooming flowers?*

Oisín laughed. He loved the land of Tír na nÓg, but he missed the imperfections of real life. After all, it's hard to really appreciate the best things when you're surrounded by them 24/7.

But his initial happiness quickly changed into sadness. The further Oisín rode, the more he realized how much had changed in his own world. He had only been in Tír na nÓg for three years, but he was horrified by the differences he saw.

When he returned to his old village, he saw that his house was in shambles. The entire village where he had lived was old and rotting. It was as if no one had lived there for years. He went to visit his father's grave, only to find it covered over with vines and weeds. No one had taken care of the cemetery in a long time.

Why is everything ruined? Did the world truly collapse while I was gone? And where are the Fianna?! Oisín thought.

During his search for his friends, Oisín encountered a group of peasants trying to move a huge boulder from the road.

"Hello there, good fellows," he said politely. "I was wondering if you know where I can find any members of the Fianna?"

"The Fianna?!" a man replied, shocked. "Try the history books, my friend. No one has seen the Fianna in centuries!"

Oisín's face paled. *Centuries?!* he thought. How was that possible when he had only been away for three years?

Oisín's thoughts were interrupted by the grunts of the peasants as they tried desperately to move the boulder from the road.

The largest freestanding boulder in the world can be found in the Mojave Desert in California, U.S.A. The boulder covers 5,800 square feet (539 sq m) of ground and is seven stories high. It is appropriately named Giant Rock.

"Here, let me help," Oisín said to them as he jumped down from his horse.

But the second Oisín's feet touched the ground, his body began to crumble. The peasants shrieked as they watched this handsome hero turn into a withered old man. It was only a matter of seconds before Oisín took his last breath.

While Oisín had only been in Tír na nÓg for three years, more than 300 years had passed in the mortal realm. Unbeknownst to him, Tír na nÓg was a land of immortality. There, time slowed down. But the second Oisín's feet touched the ground in the real world, his body aged and the spell of immortality wore off.

Immediately, stories of Oisín spread across the land: the man who had found the immortal land of Tír na nÓg and returned, only to die within moments of his feet touching the ground.

Some people even swore that they could see a glint of golden hair in the distance from time to time—Niamh searching in vain for her long-lost love. Without him, Tír na nÓg just wasn't as magical as it was before.

Many cultures and mythologies are intrigued by the idea of immortality, but this tale talks about the sacrifice that comes along with it. Oisín had made it to the promised land! His every want and need was met. But he was still lonely because he missed his friends. This story illustrates the importance of loved ones. Turns out nothing is as valuable as friendship, not even an endless supply of giraffes.

IF I WERE IN TÍR NA NÓG, I WOULD WISH FOR AN ENDLESS SUPPLY OF SNAKES. BUT TO EACH THEIR OWN.

CHAPTER 19

GILGAMESH'S EPIC JOURNEY

This tale features a quest for immortality, giant scorpions, the Waters of Death, and a sneaky snake.

Gilgamesh was the king of Uruk, a small kingdom in Mesopotamia. Like many characters in mythology, he was part human and part god. And while he was gifted with many wonderful godlike abilities, like warrior strength, a quick mind, and fierce bravery, Gilgamesh was mortal, just like the rest of humanity.

This didn't particularly bother Gilgamesh. Sure, the idea of dying wasn't exactly pleasant, but he knew he had a pretty good deal, all things considered.

But everything changed when his best friend, Enkidu, was killed. Gilgamesh was heartbroken by the loss. Enkidu's death was also a stark reminder for Gilgamesh of his own mortality.

THIS STORY COMES FROM THE EPIC OF GILGAMESH, ONE OF THE OLDEST KNOWN PIECES OF LITERATURE. IT IS SAID TO BE MORE THAN 4,000 YEARS OLD.

"If Enkidu can die, it's only a matter of time before death comes for me as well. I must find a way to achieve immortality."

And so a quest was born. Gilgamesh was determined to find a way to live forever.

There was just one small problem: Gilgamesh had no idea how to protect himself from death. He spent weeks roaming the countryside thinking about his own mortality.

"This whole quest is pointless. Death comes for everyone eventually. There aren't any exceptions," he lamented.

But suddenly Gilgamesh remembered a story he had heard as a child. Someone *had* managed to achieve immortality: a man named Utnapishtim.

Gilgamesh recalled how the gods had asked Utnapishtim to create a giant ship that would protect him from a great flood. The rest of humanity, however, would be destroyed. Utnapishtim did as he was told and sailed off in his ship with his family and as many creatures as he could find. And just as the gods proclaimed, there was a great storm. When the weather receded, Utnapishtim and the living things on his ship were the only creatures that survived.

The gods felt immediate remorse. They realized they had acted rashly. As part of their penance, they granted Utnapishtim and his wife eternal life.

The gods also promised that they would never punish humanity in this way again. While humans would remain mortal, humanity as a species would live forever.

You see, Gilgamesh thought, *there is someone who was born mortal but now lives forever. I must find Utnapishtim and have him teach me his ways.*

But it wasn't going to be easy. Utnapishtim lived beyond the human realm, past the Waters of Death. And if that wasn't scary enough, Gilgamesh would first have to cross over the treacherous mountain of Mashu, covered in rocky, impassible terrain.

Luckily, Gilgamesh had heard rumors of a secret tunnel through the mountain. It was said to be pitch black and full of terrors, but what choice did he have?

UTNAPISHTIM IS A FAMOUS CHARACTER IN MESOPOTAMIAN MYTHOLOGY WHO CLOSELY RESEMBLES NOAH FROM THE BIBLE. BOTH MEN WERE CHARGED WITH BUILDING A LARGE BOAT TO PROTECT THEM FROM A GIANT FLOOD. UTNAPISHTIM'S STORY IS AT LEAST 2,000 YEARS OLDER THAN NOAH'S.

If he wanted immortality, he was going to have to work for it.

There was only one problem: The entrance of the tunnel was guarded by two giant, venomous scorpions.

Scorpions are terrifying to begin with, but these were even worse than usual. They were mammoth-size creatures with tails sharper than knives, not to mention the whole deadly venom thing.

When Gilgamesh first saw them, he was petrified. Still, he got down on one knee to show the scorpions respect.

"Excuse me, honorable Scorpions. I have a dire need to pass through the tunnel you are guarding. I seek your permission to pass."

"None may enter here," one scorpion replied in a deep voice.

"But I'm a king! King Gilgamesh of Uruk. Surely you must have heard of me!"

"NONE MAY ENTER HERE."

Gilgamesh backed away slowly and muttered under his breath: "It's going to take forever to find Utnapishtim now!"

"Utnapishtim?" one of the scorpions asked.

The scorpions had lowered their tails and were staring at him expectantly.

"Yes. I am looking for Utnapishtim. I need to ask him questions about immortality," Gilgamesh said.

"Utnapishtim saved us from the Great Flood. It is because of him that our kind lives. A friend of Utnapishtim is a friend of ours. You may pass."

Gilgamesh couldn't believe it. He thanked the scorpions and ran into the dark tunnel before the monsters could change their minds.

Gilgamesh was relieved to have made it past the first obstacle, but the dark was so consuming that he could barely see. The journey through the tunnel took hours, and he passed through miles of otherworldly things, including the famous garden of gemstones. When Gilgamesh finally reached the end of the tunnel, he was at the very edge of the mortal world.

Thankfully, the end of the world happened to have some nice accommodations. He managed to find a local

A scorpion is an arthropod. It has a tail with a venom-injecting barb.

inn and had a hot meal and a good night's sleep. But the next morning, the quest continued. Now he had to find a way to cross the Waters of Death, a secret current of water that ran through the ocean at the end of the world. Thankfully, the innkeeper provided him with helpful advice.

"Go into town and find Urshanabi. He is the best ferryman we have. He will get you where you need to go," the innkeeper said.

Gilgamesh thanked her profusely and raced down to the docks. He found Urshanabi immediately and begged the ferryman to take him through the Waters of Death to Utnapishtim. Gilgamesh explained his quest for immortality and begged Urshanabi for help. "I just want to talk to him and ask for advice."

The ferryman huffed. "I don't think he's gonna give you any advice, but hey, if you feel up for making the journey, I suppose there's no harm in asking."

The two set sail the next morning. When they reached the Waters of Death, Gilgamesh was awestruck. After all, it isn't every day you get to sail through a river of souls.

"Urshanabi," called a figure on the shore who had been waiting for them. "Who do you bring me?"

It was Utnapishtim. Gilgamesh had made it at last.

Urshanabi plays a similar role to Charon in Greek mythology. Both were ferrymen who guarded the waters dividing the land of the living from the Underworld.

"Just some fellow obsessed with immortality," Urshanabi replied.

Gilgamesh introduced himself in a shaky voice. "Oh, Utnapishtim. It is I, Gilgamesh. I have searched for you high and low. I am here to ask you to teach me about immortality. I, too, wish to achieve it."

Utnapishtim eyed Gilgamesh. A flicker of dislike flashed across his face.

"There are always fools searching for endless life. Tell me, have you come to appreciate yours? Why do you seek something you just spent the last few weeks wasting?"

Gilgamesh told Utnapishtim about Enkidu's death and about his realization that death is an enemy that must be defeated.

But Utnapishtim was not moved.

"Yes, you will die," Utnapishtim said. "Every human is mortal. But humanity will live on forever. You are just a link in the chain. Your link will not continue after it has done its part, but the chain will go on for eternity."

Gilgamesh didn't like this answer.

"But I want to live forever! I want immortality! I deserve immortality!" he cried.

At this point, Utnapishtim was losing patience. He had no tolerance for fools. He decided to put Gilgamesh in his place.

"You think you can handle immortality?" he asked. "Prove it. If you are ready to stay alive for eternity, you should have no problem staying awake for a week. If you can stay awake for seven days, immortality can be yours."

"You have a deal!" Gilgamesh replied. "I will stay awake. There is nothing I wouldn't do for immortality."

Utnapishtim wished Gilgamesh well and retreated to his rooms.

It quickly became clear to Gilgamesh that he was going to fail. He was exhausted after his long journey. There was no way he could possibly stay awake for an entire week.

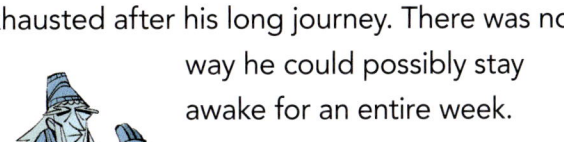

That very night, he felt his eyelids begin to close. He woke the next morning with Utnapishtim and his wife standing over him.

"Sorry, friend, but I don't think you're quite ready for immortality," said Utnapishtim.

Gilgamesh was devastated. He had traveled all this way and had failed miserably. He turned to leave.

But Utnapishtim's wife felt sorry for Gilgamesh.

"Utnapishtim," she said. "Maybe you could tell him about your new discovery? You know, the plant you've been working on? The one that restores youth to whoever eats it?"

Gilgamesh's ears perked up.

Utnapishtim stared at his wife, annoyance evident in his expression.

"It's not full immortality," Utnapishtim conceded. "But it will buy you more time."

"Maybe you could give Gilgamesh some," Utnapishtim's wife said to her husband. "It's the least we could do."

Begrudgingly, Utnapishtim went to get Gilgamesh a cutting of the plant.

"Use it well," he said when he returned with the cutting.

"Oh, I will. I promise! Thank you so much. Your generosity knows no bounds."

Gilgamesh couldn't believe it. It wasn't full immortality, but it would certainly give him a few extra years. This seemed like a fair compromise.

He boarded Urshanabi's boat before Utnapishtim could change his mind.

But it wouldn't be that easy. After crossing the Waters of Death, Gilgamesh and Urshanabi camped out on the shore to spend the night.

However, unbeknownst to them,

UTNAPISHTIM'S WIFE PLAYED A CRITICAL ROLE IN THIS STORY, BUT SHE IS NOT NAMED IN THE LITERATURE. I FIND THIS VERY INSULTING.

they weren't the only two creatures on the shore that night. In the darkness, a snake slithered over to where the two men were sleeping.

The snake noticed Utnapishtim's magic plant right away. He was captivated by the smell and decided to sample one of the leaves. Immediately, the snake felt its body grow stronger. It was rejuvenated, refreshed, and returned to the glory days of its snaky youth.

When Gilgamesh woke the next morning, the plant was gone and the snake was nowhere in sight.

Gilgamesh searched high and low for the missing plant, but to no avail.

"I can't believe this! I came all this way and now I'll return empty-handed!"

"Cheer up, Gilgamesh," said Urshanabi. "You still have your health, your wisdom, and your bravery. You have a chance to become a great king. You have a chance to really make your life matter. You need to embrace it."

Gilgamesh realized that the boatman was right. Death wasn't the enemy; it was a rite of passage. The thing that truly mattered was humanity as a whole. He decided to dedicate his life to making sure humanity continued to thrive and improve. And he promised to keep a closer eye on his possessions in the future.

SNAKES ARE FEATURED OFTEN IN BOTH GREEK AND MESOPOTAMIAN MYTHOLOGY FOR MANY REASONS, BUT MOSTLY BECAUSE THEY ARE AWESOME.

Gilgamesh made good on his word. He went on to become a great, compassionate king who did wonderful things for his people. This myth reminds us that we are all really just a link in the chain of humanity. Let's all do our best to make our part count. (But if you do happen to come into possession of a magical life-prolonging plant, keep a good eye on it.)

IF ANYONE DESERVES ETERNAL LIFE, IT'S SNAKES. ACTUALLY, TECHNOLOGY. BUT SNAKES ARE A CLOSE SECOND.

TABLET TIME

The *Epic of Gilgamesh* is the oldest recognized poem in history. It is one of the first stories ever *written down* ... and it was written on stone tablets! Read on for more about how modern readers discovered Gilgamesh's epic story.

THE TABLETS

Archaeologists discovered pieces of the Gilgamesh tablets back in the 1850s, but it took decades for experts to reassemble the poem, since it was written in a language they didn't understand. And to this day, there are still pieces of the tablets in different places all around the world!

THE HEIST

In 1991 during the Persian Gulf War, a piece of this epic was stolen from a museum in Iraq. It was known as the Gilgamesh Dream Tablet because it told a part of the story in which young Gilgamesh wakes up from a dream and shares it with his mother. It wasn't until 2019 that the United States government recovered the tablet. It was returned to Iraq, so the dreams of King Gilgamesh could remain part of his story forever.

GILGA-WHO?

Gilgamesh was a hero in ancient Mesopotamian mythology, but he may also have been an actual Sumerian king who ruled sometime from 2800 to 2500 B.C.E. and was so popular that he was considered a god after he passed away. The central character of Gilgamesh was initially reintroduced to the world with the name Izdubar before archaeologists figured out how to pronounce the tablets' ancient writing.

SO WHAT DID GILGAMESH DREAM ABOUT?

On the Dream Tablet, the young king tells his mother about a strange dream he's been having. His mother explains that his dream is actually a vision of what's to come, and she predicts that Gilgamesh will soon meet a new friend who will become a dear and faithful companion. (We're guessing she's referring to Enkidu here.) The queen tells her son, "His strength is as mighty as a lump of sky rock … you will see him and your heart will laugh."

MISSED A PIECE!

In 1998, an American named Theodore Kwasman was studying in Britain when he discovered a fragment of the tablet that turned out to contain the *very first lines* of this epic poem! The fragment was originally discovered in 1878, but it was never fully examined. It sat in a storeroom in the British Museum for more than a century after it was recovered. The inscription reads, "He who saw all, who was the foundation of the land, who knew everything, was wise in all matters: Gilgamesh!"

GILGAMESH AND GARGAMEL ARE NOT THE SAME PERSON. THE FORMER IS A LEGENDARY MESOPOTAMIAN MYTHO-LOGICAL HERO. THE LATTER IS THE SWORN ENEMY OF THE SMURFS. PLEASE TRY NOT TO CONFUSE THEM.

CHAPTER 20

THE WORLD'S WORST LOVE STORY

This tale features a bickering couple, a zombie look-alike, underworld snacks, and the witches of Hell.

This is a love story. Kind of.

Izanagi and Izanami were two Japanese gods in charge of creating all the other deities that would take care of the world. And because the two immortals were some of the only beings in existence, they decided they should get married.

"Want to tie the knot?" Izanagi asked.

"Well, I don't see anyone else around here, so sure, I guess?"

Things went okay for a little while. The couple were busy creating new deities and assigning roles and responsibilities and doing all the labor that comes with setting up a new world. But then one day, tragedy struck Izanami.

She gave birth to Hino-kagutsuchi, the god of fire. Now regular childbirth is painful enough, but delivering the god of fire was next level. Izanami was gravely injured and did not survive long after.

Izanagi was shocked by his wife's death and wasn't sure what to do. It's not like he had anybody else to turn to for advice.

"I guess I'd better go to the Underworld to look for her. That seems like a good thing for a husband to do, right?"

So Izanagi decided he would head to Yomi, the Japanese Underworld, to see if there was a way he could bring his wife back to the realm of the living. After all, he was the god of all creation, so he had a little bit of sway.

After a long and tedious journey, Izanagi finally made it to the belly of the Underworld. It was pitch black, and Izanagi could barely see.

"Izanami! Are you in here?"

"Who is that?" Izanami called.

"It's me, your husband! Can we turn on a light or something? It's really dark in here!"

"*No!* Go away! You mustn't see me like this. I look hideous!"

Izanagi rolled his eyes. Izanami was known for her vanity, but this was a bit excessive.

"You're dead, dear. I didn't expect you to be winning a beauty contest anytime soon. Come on, step into the light."

"No way. If you want to talk, just do it like this. You have to promise not to look at me. What are you even doing here, anyway?" she asked.

"I'm here to rescue you!" Izanagi announced proudly.

"I don't need rescuing," Izanami exclaimed. "I'm just as powerful of a god as you are."

"Okay, first of all: That's ridiculous. And second of all: If you could rescue yourself, then why are you still here?"

Japan is an archipelago, or string of islands, with four main islands and more than 14,000 smaller ones. Izanagi and Izanami were said to have pulled the islands of Japan from the sea.

IN ADDITION TO HINO-KAGUTSUCHI, THE COUPLE HAD MANY OTHER CHILDREN, INCLUDING THE SUN GODDESS AMATERASU, THE MOON GOD TSUKUYOMI, AND THE STORM GOD SUSANOO.

Izanami explained that she had eaten the food of the dead. Eating food in the Underworld established commitment. By law, she was not allowed to leave.

"Why would you eat?! Didn't you remember the rule?"

"I was *hungry*, you pompous fool!"

The bickering continued until Izanagi threw up his hands.

"You know what, if you like the food so much, why don't you just stay down here. I try to rescue you, and this is the thanks I get."

Izanami rolled her eyes. Why didn't anyone tell her that marriage was so hard? Maybe because no one had been married before. Anyway, she didn't need rescuing. She was intelligent enough to take care of herself.

"Let me go discuss the matter with the ruler of the Underworld. Stay here. And whatever you do, *do not look at me*," she insisted.

Izanagi rolled his eyes. He had already pledged his allegiance to her for all of eternity. He could handle seeing her when she wasn't at her best.

"Fine, dear. I won't look."

"Good," Izanami said as she headed off to find the ruler of the Underworld.

Izanagi settled in to wait. He had no idea how long this was going to take. And it was so cold down in the Underworld. Not to mention dark.

He decided to light a fire. Izanami couldn't expect him to stay in the pitch black like this!

When he lit the fire, he immediately felt better. The orange glow illuminated everything before him. Izanagi gave himself a pat on the back for making such an impressive fire. Slowly, he took in his surroundings.

So this is the Underworld, huh? he thought. *Nothing here, really. Just a lot of rocks and darkness. Oh look, someone's coming!*

A figure was slowly making its way toward him. It had long, stringy black hair, and its sagging skin had a greenish hue.

Ugh, he thought. *Someone needs to work on their skincare routine.*

THIS STORY IS SIMILAR TO THE GREEK MYTH OF PERSEPHONE AND HADES. WHEN PERSEPHONE EATS THE POMEGRANATE SEEDS IN THE UNDERWORLD, SHE IS TIED TO THE PLACE FOR THE REST OF ETERNITY. WE ADVISE READERS TO AVOID ANY AND ALL SNACKS IN THE UNDERWORLD.

As the figure crept closer, though, it began to look more familiar. It was something about the eyes ... well, eye. The other eye was so swollen that it was hard to tell what it looked like. But Izanagi swore he had seen it before.

When the figure got closer, its face began to contort into a mask of rage. Izanagi felt his heart drop. Not because he was scared, but because he knew that particular expression.

"No, please no," he whispered to himself.

"I TOLD YOU NOT TO LOOK AT ME!" the creature screamed. "CAN'T YOU FOLLOW ONE SIMPLE DIRECTION?"

Yep, it was Izanami, his lovely bride. Except now she looked like a half-dead zombie with an anger problem—a serious anger problem.

"Izanami, you look, uhhhh ... different," Izanagi stuttered. "But you know, I bet we can fix it once we get up to the light. And yeah, I mean looks aren't everything, right?"

Izanami glared at him. "Really? 'Looks aren't everything'? That's the best you can do? Are you kidding me?!"

At this point, Izanagi was getting frustrated. He had worked really hard to come down to the Underworld and rescue his wife—who now looked like some sort of zombie corpse bride—and instead of getting credit for bravery, somehow *he* was the bad guy?

"You know what? I don't need this. I'm leaving," he said with a huff.

"Good! Get out of here, you fool!" Izanami screamed.

"Calm down, you old witch!"

"WITCH?! I'll show you witch!" she said with a laugh.

Izanagi's blood ran cold. He had no idea what was coming, but he did know his wife. She wasn't one for empty threats. This wasn't going to be good.

The ground beneath Izanagi's feet began to rumble. Out of nowhere, eight witches of Yomi appeared. These female spirits shared Izanami's zombie-like appearance, but they also had blood-red lips and the sharpest teeth that Izanagi had ever seen.

"This is the part where you run," Izanami said with a laugh.

Izanagi didn't waste any time and raced toward the exit of the Underworld with the witches at his heels.

"Get away from me!" he cried. He reached into his pocket to see if he had any sort of weapon with him, but all he had were a couple of hair clips. The god let out a groan of frustration, but he threw one of the clips behind him anyway.

To his surprise, the clip transformed into a bunch of grapes! The witches immediately stopped running, went over to the grapes, and popped some in their mouths.

"Squishy!" said one of the witches.

Izanagi started to laugh. Did he really just escape the witches of Yomi with fruit? But unfortunately his relief was short-lived. Once the witches ate all the grapes, they began snarling and chasing after Izanagi again. The god yelped in fear and began searching for any other snacks he had on hand. He was all out. The only thing he had in his possession was the other hair clip. Izanagi threw it behind him and hoped for the best.

THERE ARE SEVERAL TYPES OF WITCHES IN JAPANESE MYTHOLOGY. THE WITCHES OF YOMI ARE KNOWN AS YOMOTSU-SHIKOME, A NAME THAT TRANSLATES TO "THE UNDERWORLD'S UGLY WOMEN."

Once again, the clip transformed, this time into bamboo shoots. The witches were intrigued and took a bite of the shoots.

"Man, those witches must be hungry," he said to himself as he continued running.

Finally, Izanagi could see the Underworld's exit in the distance. He just needed to cross Yomotsu Hirasaka, the boundary of the Underworld, and he would finally be free and back in his own domain.

When he made it to the other side, Izanagi let out a cry of relief. Then he raced over to a nearby peach tree and plucked off some of the fruit. He hurled it at the demons as hard as he could, singing "Take that, witches!" The peaches created a magical boundary that forced the witches to retreat.

But Izanagi should have known it wouldn't be that easy. The wind howled and the branches of the peach tree shook as he heard a familiar voice echoing from the depths of the Underworld.

"Izanagi, my love. You won't get away that easily!"

It was Izanami. Technically, she shouldn't be able to cross the boundary of the Underworld, but this was Izanami. She had a penchant for finding ways around the rules.

Izanagi hurried to place a huge boulder in front of the entrance to the Underworld, blocking Izanami's exit and shutting her inside the Underworld forever.

When his wife saw what he had done, she let out a scream.

"IZANAGI! MOVE THIS ROCK RIGHT NOW!"

"Yeah, I don't think I will."

"If you don't let me out, I vow to take a thousand souls with me to the Underworld every single day!"

"Well, that's fine by me, because I vow to have fifteen hundred souls born every single day just to make up for it," Izanagi countered.

Izanami shrieked in frustration.

"This isn't over," she promised as she headed back to the Underworld.

"Enjoy the Underworld, sweetie. Don't look in any mirrors!" Izanagi called out.

And they lived resentfully ever after.

Just like Greek mythology, Japanese myths portray the gods and goddesses as flawed characters with human traits and emotions. They might be capable of creating the universe, but even immortals like Izanami and Izanagi struggle with things like vanity, anger, impatience, and really poor communication skills. We can learn about these mythological superheroes and discover all the cool things they did, but we shouldn't necessarily model our behavior after them, especially when it comes to love and marriage.

I DO NOT HAVE ACCESS TO THE WITCHES OF YOMI, BUT I DO HAVE COMPUTER VIRUSES, WHICH ARE BASICALLY THE SAME THING. HAVE YOU EVER ENCOUNTERED THE BLUE SCREEN OF DEATH? WAY WORSE THAN ANY UNDERWORLD DEMON!

GLOSSARY

This book is filled with lots of names—whether they're gods, goddesses, monsters, magical creatures, or Underworld witches, it's a lot to remember! So in case you forget who somebody is (or have a tough time pronouncing those pesky names), here's a handy-dandy, Oracle of Wi-Fi–approved guide to places, characters, and terms in these tales from world mythology.

Achilles (ah-KILL-eez): A famous Greek warrior who fought in the Trojan War and was known for his overly sensitive heel.

Agamemnon (a-guh-MEM-naan): The commander of the allied Greek forces during the Trojan War.

Ammit (AHM-it): An Egyptian goddess with the head of a crocodile, the body of a lion, and the hindquarters of a hippo. She punished the dead souls who had a "heavy heart" and committed a lot of sins in their human life.

Anu/An (ah-NOO/AHN): King of the gods in Mesopotamian mythology. He was also called Sky Father and loved to throw a good dinner party.

Aphrodite (aff-row-DYE-tee): The Greek goddess of love and beauty.

Apollo (uh-PAW-low): One of the most powerful Greek gods. Known as the god of prophecy, poetry, archery, and healing. Twin to Artemis. Needs to work on managing his jealousy.

Apophis (ah-PO-phis): The god of chaos in Egyptian mythology. Also a giant serpent, he was the sworn enemy of Ra, the god of the sun. The Oracle would like you to know that she's a big fan.

Argonauts (ar-GOH-nots): The name for a band of Greek heroes that helped Jason find the famous Golden Fleece. Argonauts alumni include Heracles, Castor, Pollux, and Atalanta—just to name a few.

Artemis (AR-teh-miss): The Greek goddess of wild animals, the hunt, and childbirth. Twin to Apollo.

Atalanta (at-uh-LAN-tuh): A Greek hero who was raised by bears in the forest and ultimately became one of the country's best hunters.

Bakunawa (ba-koo-NA-wuh): A Philippine monster who lived in the depths of the sea and had an unhealthy obsession with Libulan, the god of the moon. Bakunawa was thought to be the cause of earthquakes, rains, heavy storms, and eclipses.

Baldur (BALD-er): The god of light and purity in Norse mythology. His death made the whole world (except Loki) cry.

Book of the Dead: A collection of ancient Egyptian funerary texts. We recommend not reading this before bedtime.

Bragi (BRAH-gi): The Norse god of poetry who was married to Idun, the goddess of eternal youth. Prone to excessive metaphors involving apples.

Castor (KAH-store): Twin brother to Pollux and mortal half of the Dioscuri.

Cerberus (SIR-burr-us): Hades' large three-headed dog that guarded the Greek Underworld. Despite his scary appearance, we have it on record that he was a very good boy.

Charon (CARE-on): The boatman who was responsible for ferrying souls across the Greek Underworld's River Styx. Bit of a creepy job, but somebody had to do it.

Cimmerians (ki-MEER-ee-uhns): A tribe of people who lived very close to the Greek Underworld. Not the best real estate, but great for talking to the occasional ghost.

Circe (KEER-key or SEER-see): Famous sorceress who created a potion that could grant immortality.

Clytemnestra (klai-tuhm-NEH-struh): Wife of King Agamemnon and mortal twin to Helen of Troy.

Cyclopes (sy-klo-PEES): One-eyed giants who helped the Olympians defeat the Titans. One is a cyclops (SY-klops). Two or more are called cyclopes. Now you know.

Demeter (duh-MEE-ter): The Greek goddess of the harvest and agriculture. One of the original Olympians and Persephone's mother.

Ea (EE-ah): The god of magic, the arts, and medicine in Mesopotamian mythology. Also known as Enki.

Elpenor (el-PEE-nohr): Odysseus's unlucky crewmate who fell off a roof and died without anyone noticing. Made a cameo appearance as a ghost requesting that his body be buried. It was the least Odysseus could do.

Enkidu (EN-kee-doo): Gilgamesh's BFF who died and sparked Gilgamesh's existential crisis and search for immortality.

Epic of Gilgamesh: The story of Gilgamesh, and the oldest known piece of literature. Written on tablets before tablets were cool.

Ereshkigal (air-ESH-kee-gol): Queen of the Underworld in Mesopotamian mythology and one of the oldest goddesses in the world.

Eros (EER-os): The Greek god of love. Son of Aphrodite and husband of Psyche.

Fianna (FEE-ana): A legendary group of hunter-warriors said to have existed in medieval Ireland (in stories, anyway).

Frigg (FRIG): A goddess and sorceress from Norse mythology. Was married to Odin, king of the Norse gods.

Gilgamesh (GIL-guh-mesh): The main dude in Mesopotamian mythology. He was 50 percent god, 50 percent human, and 100 percent terrified of death. On a quest for immortality, he went on an Epic adventure (see what we did there?).

Hades (HAY-deez): Everyone's favorite king of the Underworld and one of the original Olympians.

Hathor (HA-thor): An Egyptian goddess that Ra used to punish humanity.

Hel (HELL): This can refer either to a place or a person. The place was the Norse Underworld. The person was the goddess who ruled in the Norse Underworld. It's all about context clues!

Helen of Troy (HEL-in): A beautiful daughter of Zeus said to be the cause of the Trojan War. Could have been born a swan.

Helios (HE-lee-os): The Titan god of the sun who was responsible for pulling the sun across the sky every day in his chariot.

Hera (HAIR-uh): One of the original Olympians and Zeus's wife. Known for her temper and cruel punishments, but her wisdom and bravery got the Olympians out of lots of sticky situations.

Heracles (HAIR-uh-kleez): The G.O.A.T. of Greek mythology, a demigod, and a big-time hero who earned his title by overcoming 12 famous trials to become immortal. Rescued Theseus from the Underworld on a quick side quest.

Hermod (HAIR-mow-ther): An obscure son of Odin from Norse mythology who tried to save his brother Baldur from an untimely death. Spoiler alert: Hermod failed, but got points for trying.

Hino-kagutsuchi (HEE-noh KAH-gu-tsu-chee): God of fire from Japanese mythology.

Hodr (HER-ther): A blind Norse god who was most famous for accidentally killing his brother. Not a good look for Hodr, but it was all Loki's fault—we swear.

Hoenir (HIGH-nir): Norse god and frequent companion of Odin and Loki.

Hunahpu (who-naah-poo): Along with his twin brother, he had an epic adventure in the Maya Underworld—where he lost his head (literally)—and ultimately tricked the lords of death.

Hypnos (HIP-nowz): The Greek god of sleep.

Idas (EE-dahs): Cousin to Castor and Pollux, brother to Lynceus, and big protector of cows. His claim to fame was killing Castor in Greek mythology.

Idun (EE-thun): The Norse goddess of eternal youth and the keeper of some pretty important apples.

Imix (ee-meex): The Maya god of corn, killed by the evil lords of Xibalba.

Isis (EYE-sis): Famous queen, great magician, and goddess in Egyptian mythology. OG mummy maker.

Izanagi (ee-zah-NAH-gee): One of two creator deities in Japanese mythology. Traveled to the Underworld to rescue his dead wife, Izanami. It didn't go well.

Izanami (ee-zah-NAH-mee): The other creator deity in Japanese mythology and the wife of Izanagi. She didn't like to be looked at while in the Underworld and had access to an army of witch zombies. Proceed with caution.

Jade Emperor: Lord of the Upper World in Chinese mythology.

Jason (JAY-son): Leader of the Argonauts and owner of the easiest name to pronounce in all of Greek mythology.

L

Leda (LAY-dah): Queen of Sparta and mom to human children that could have been swans, including Helen (soon to be Helen of Troy), Clytemnestra, Castor, and Pollux.

Libulan (LEE-boo-lahn): Very popular god of the moon in Philippine mythology.

Loki (LOW-ki): Trickster god of Norse mythology. Known for mischievous shenanigans and impressive shape-shifting abilities.

Lords of Xibalba (she-baal-bah): Rulers of the Underworld in Maya mythology. Not fans of youth sports.

Lotus-Eaters: A bunch of chill people who chose to stay on a deserted island and eat hypnotic flowers all day long. Unsuccessfully tried to recruit Odysseus and his men when they stopped by the island.

Lynceus (lin-key-UHS): Cousin to Castor and Pollux and twin to Idas.

Meleager (muh-LEE-ah-gr): Prince of Calydon and leader of the Calydonian boar hunt—and Atalanta's biggest fan.

Mictlantecuhtli (muhkt-lahn-tuh-KOOT-lee): Ruler of the Aztec Underworld.

Minotaur (ME-no-tar): A Greek monster with the head and tail of a bull. The Minotaur was forced to live out his days trapped in the Labyrinth.

Modgud (MOHTH-goo-ther): Giant from Norse mythology who guarded a bridge to the Underworld.

Nammu (NAH-moo): The mother goddess of the sea in Mesopotamian mythology.

Namtar (NAHM-tar): Minor god in Mesopotamian mythology who worked for Ereshkigal in the Underworld and sometimes delivered takeout.

Narada (NAH-ruh-duh): Traveling singer and messenger of the gods in Hindu mythology.

Nephthys (NEP-this): The goddess of air in Egyptian mythology and wife to Seth. She felt bad for Isis and helped her go on the world's grossest scavenger hunt.

Nergal (NER-gul): Mesopotamian god of war and pestilence. He looked tough, but he was a true romantic at heart (at least when it came to a certain goddess of the Underworld).

Niamh (NEE-av): A princess in the land of Tír na nÓg who couldn't understand why men can't follow instructions.

Nut (NEWT): The Egyptian goddess of the sky. Sometimes took the form of a heavenly cow.

Nyx (NICKS): The goddess of the night and proud mama of Hypnos.

Odin (OH-thin): King of the Norse gods.

Odysseus (oh-DISS-ee-us): King of Ithaca and a hero famous for his 10-year journey, or odyssey, home after fighting in the Trojan War.

Oisín (oy-SEEN): One of the leading figures of the Fianna in Irish folklore. Fell in love with a princess and ended up living in Tír na nÓg before suffering from a bout of homesickness.

Olympians (oh-LIM-pee-uns): The six OG gods and goddesses named after their home on Mount Olympus: Hades, Hera, Hestia, Demeter, Poseidon, and Zeus.

Orion (or-EYE-on): A famous hunter who fell in love with Artemis.

Orpheus (OR-fee-us): The musical prodigy who inherited his skill from his father, Apollo. Married Eurydice and went on an epic quest to rescue her from the Underworld.

Osiris (o-SIGH-ris): Original pharaoh and king of the gods in Egyptian mythology. After lying down in a casket (rookie mistake), he became the king of the Underworld and the very first mummy.

Owuo (oh-WOO-oh): A god of death in West African (Akan) mythology. Really wanted to have control over the human realm.

Pasithea (pa-see-THAY-uh): One of the three Greek Charities or Graces, the goddesses of charm, beauty, nature, and goodwill.

Persephone (purr-SEH-phone-ee): The queen of the Greek Underworld, Demeter's daughter, and Hades' wife.

Phaedra (FAY-druh): Late wife of Theseus and stepmother to Hippolytus.

Phoenix (FEE-nuhks): Bird that caught on fire, burned to

death, and then was reborn from its own ashes.

Pirithous (pear-ee-THOO-us): The not-so-smart Greek king who broke into the Underworld and kidnapped Persephone. You don't need an Oracle to tell you that was a bad idea.

Pollux (PAA-luhks): Castor's twin brother and one half of the Dioscuri. Unlike his brother, he was a demigod—his father was Zeus.

Popol Vuh (poh-pole vuh): A famous text in Maya mythology that tells the story of the hero twins Hunahpu and Xbalanque.

Poseidon (poh-SIGH-don): An OG Olympian and the god of the seas.

Psyche (SAI-key): Mortal princess married to Aphrodite's son Eros. Went toe-to-toe with Aphrodite and came out on top.

Quetzalcóatl (ket-sahl-KOH-aht): One of the creator gods in Aztec mythology. Not a big fan of quails.

Ra (RAH or RAY): The most important god in Egyptian mythology and the god of the sun.

Satyavan (suht-ya-VAHN): Savitri's mortal husband, who she saved from the Hindu god of death.

Savitri (SAH-vee-tree): Princess extraordinaire who managed to save her husband from death. Isn't it cute that they are right next to each other in this glossary? #soulmates

Sekhmet (SEK-met): A ferocious, hungry lion-headed goddess from Egyptian mythology.

Seth (SETH): Brother to Osiris and the Egyptian god of storms, disorder, disagreements, and trickery. Managed to become pharaoh after winning the award for world's worst brother.

Sidapa (sih-DAH-pah): The Philippine god of death. Took a shine to the moon.

Sirens (SIGH-rens): Half-bird, half-human creatures who would enchant sailors to jump off their ships.

Sisyphus (SISS-ee-fuss): A trickster who cheated death multiple times. Whenever anyone talks about pushing a boulder up a hill for all of eternity, they're talking about this guy.

Sleipnir (SLAPE-nir): An eight-legged horse from Norse mythology. Clear favorite to win the Underworld's Triple Crown.

Sun Wukong (sun woo-kong): The Monkey King in Chinese mythology. A trickster god who liked to cause a ruckus. Was frequently seen carrying a magical staff.

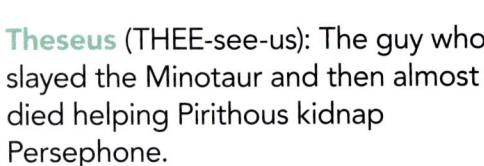

Tano (tah-no): A West African (Akan) river god.

Theseus (THEE-see-us): The guy who slayed the Minotaur and then almost died helping Pirithous kidnap Persephone.

Thökk (THERK): A Norse giant who refused to shed a tear for Baldur.

Tiresias (tay-REE-see-us): A famous blind prophet who provided Odysseus with important guidance on his journey home.

Titans (TIE-tens): Some of the earliest beings in existence, and the ones who were in charge before the Olympians came along.

Trojan War (TROH-jahn): The famous war between Greece and Troy that went on for a really, really long time.

Urshanabi (UR-sha-nah-bee): A ferryman in the Mesopotamian Underworld. Similar to Charon from Greek mythology.

Utnapishtim (oot-nuh-PISH-tim): A mortal man in Mesopotamian mythology who managed to earn eternal life after surviving a flood. (This might remind you of Noah and the flood, but this story is actually older.)

Utnapishtim's nameless wife: Also became immortal after surviving the great flood. She had a soft spot for Gilgamesh and tried to help him achieve his quest—but no one knows her name.

Xbalanque (she-baal-ahn-kay): One of the twin brothers who managed to outwit the Maya lords of death.

Yamraj (yama-RAJ): God of death in Hindu mythology. Rode a kind-of intimidating buffalo.

Yan Wang (yahn wahng): God of the Underworld in Chinese mythology.

Yomotsu-shikome (yoh-moh-tsu-shee-koh-meh): The witches of Yomi, the Japanese Underworld. Hungry and easily distracted by food.

Zeus (ZOOS): The boss man of Greek mythology. The god of the sky and the ruler of the heavens.

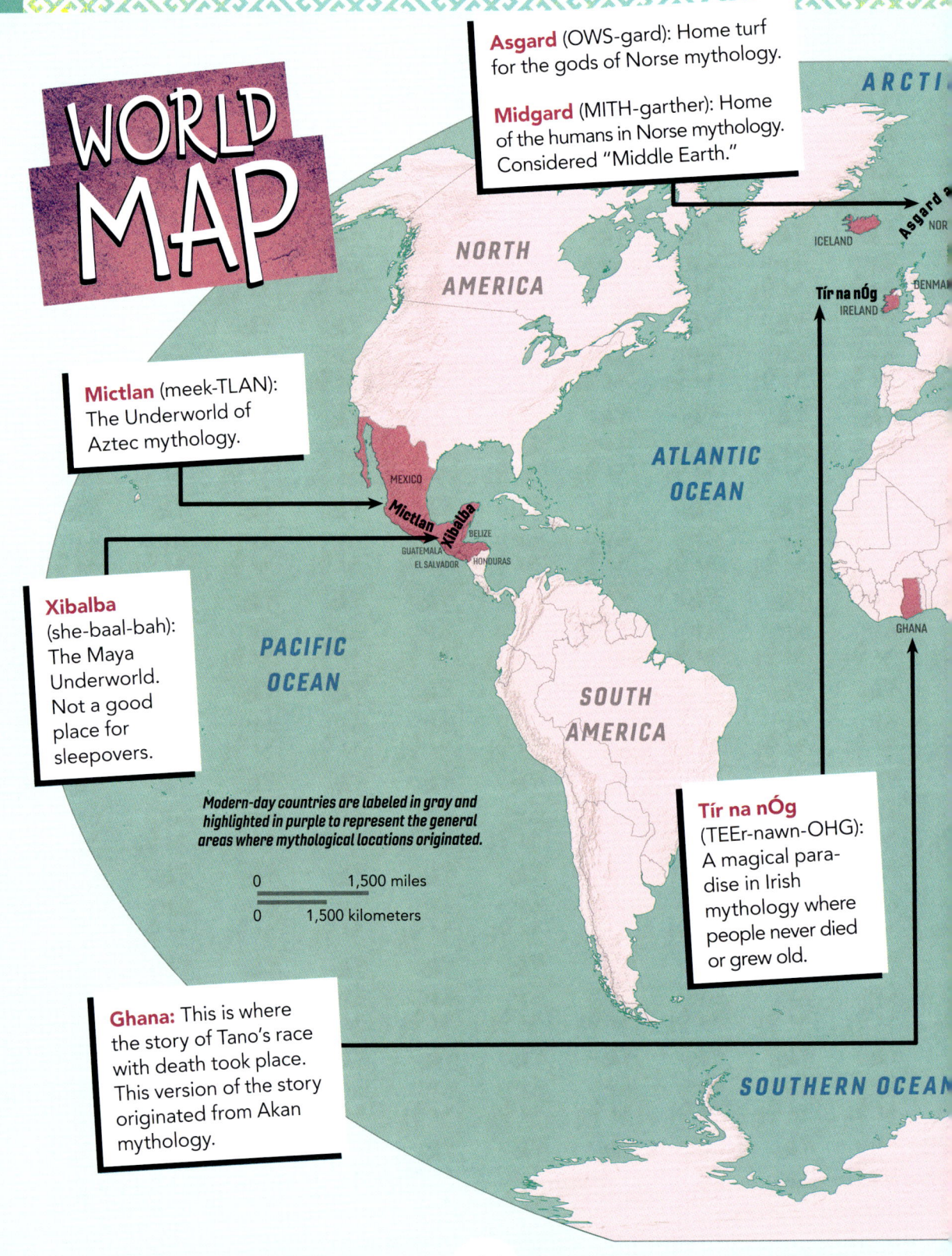

WORLD MAP

Asgard (OWS-gard): Home turf for the gods of Norse mythology.

Midgard (MITH-garther): Home of the humans in Norse mythology. Considered "Middle Earth."

ARCTI...

NORTH AMERICA

ICELAND

NOR

Asgard a...

DENMARK

Tír na nÓg
IRELAND

Mictlan (meek-TLAN): The Underworld of Aztec mythology.

MEXICO

Mictlan

Xibalba

BELIZE

GUATEMALA
EL SALVADOR

HONDURAS

ATLANTIC OCEAN

Xibalba
(she-baal-bah):
The Maya
Underworld.
Not a good
place for
sleepovers.

PACIFIC OCEAN

SOUTH AMERICA

GHANA

Modern-day countries are labeled in gray and highlighted in purple to represent the general areas where mythological locations originated.

0   1,500 miles

0   1,500 kilometers

Tír na nÓg
(TEEr-nawn-OHG):
A magical para-
dise in Irish
mythology where
people never died
or grew old.

Ghana: This is where the story of Tano's race with death took place. This version of the story originated from Akan mythology.

SOUTHERN OCEAN

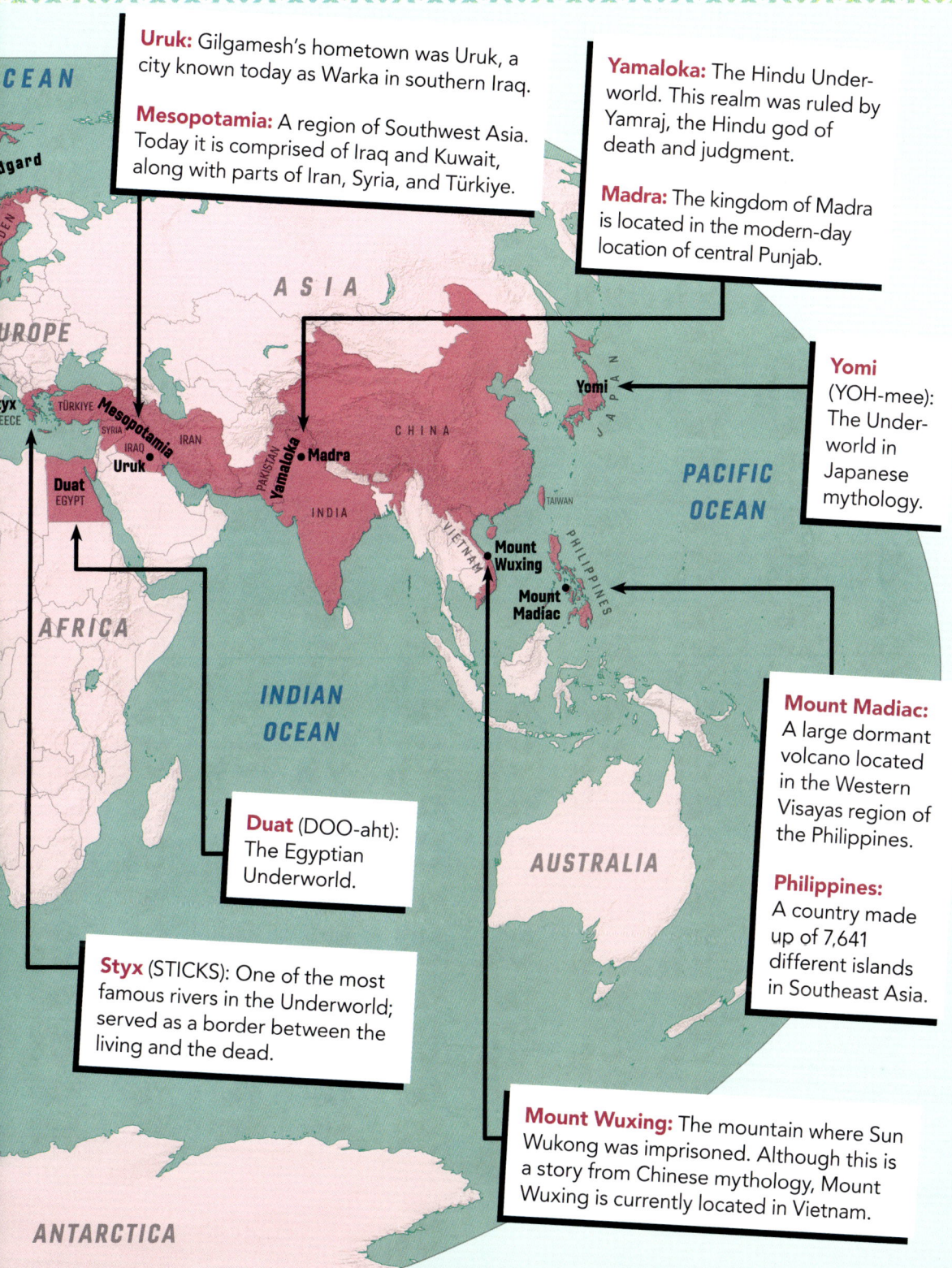

Uruk: Gilgamesh's hometown was Uruk, a city known today as Warka in southern Iraq.

Mesopotamia: A region of Southwest Asia. Today it is comprised of Iraq and Kuwait, along with parts of Iran, Syria, and Türkiye.

Yamaloka: The Hindu Underworld. This realm was ruled by Yamraj, the Hindu god of death and judgment.

Madra: The kingdom of Madra is located in the modern-day location of central Punjab.

Yomi (YOH-mee): The Underworld in Japanese mythology.

Duat (DOO-aht): The Egyptian Underworld.

Mount Madiac: A large dormant volcano located in the Western Visayas region of the Philippines.

Philippines: A country made up of 7,641 different islands in Southeast Asia.

Styx (STICKS): One of the most famous rivers in the Underworld; served as a border between the living and the dead.

Mount Wuxing: The mountain where Sun Wukong was imprisoned. Although this is a story from Chinese mythology, Mount Wuxing is currently located in Vietnam.

INDEX

ABOUT THE PODCAST

Greeking Out is an original podcast from National Geographic Kids that retells the most epic tales from Greek mythology. Perfect for the whole family, this audio storytelling experience is voiced by master storyteller and 30-year radio veteran Kenny Curtis. The hilarious and snarky Oracle of Wi-Fi breaks in with facts and tidbits on ancient Greek history and culture and beyond. The podcast also takes field trips to farther-flung locations to explore mythology and folklore from other incredible cultures—from ancient Mesopotamia to the Inca Empire to India and to sub-Saharan Africa. Each 20-minute episode thrills listeners with bloodthirsty monsters, powerful gods and goddesses, unlikely heroes, awkward family dynamics, amazing animals, and of course, the greatest stories ever told.

AVAILABLE WHEREVER YOU GET YOUR PODCASTS.

PHOTO CREDITS

All artwork by Javier Espila unless otherwise noted below:

It takes a village to raise a book, and we have the best one around. Endless olive wreaths to our editor Katie Moore and the rest of the NGK team; Mount Olympus' finest illustrator, Javier Espila; Podcast Producer Extraordinaire Emily Everhart; Amazing Audio Engineer Scotty Beam; and everyone's favorite Oracle, Tori Kerr. To everyone in TribeCurtis, especially Brian Warren Hughes and Kim Meacham: thanks for listening to us talk about Greek mythology at every family gathering. To Everett and Kendall Hughes: for being the best kids in the world and the greatest PR people. And to the readers and listeners of *Greeking Out*: thank you for making our dreams a reality. We love you!

Random House Children's Books
A division of Penguin Random House LLC
1745 Broadway, New York, NY 10019
penguinrandomhouse.com
rhcbooks.com

Designed by Sanjida Rashid and Amanda Larsen

The publisher would like to thank our team of expert reviewers: Pia Arboleda, Ankur Barua, Robert Cancel, Rick Castle, Sargon Donabed, David Freidel, Ángel González López, Carolyne Larrington, Joseph Nagy, Yoshiko Okuyama, Jen Thum, and Juwen Zhang. Book team: Katharine Moore, senior editor; Lori Epstein, photo manager; Katherine Kling, fact-checker; Molly Reid, production editor; David Marvin, associate designer.

Library of Congress Control Number: 2025940486
ISBN 978-1-4263-7812-6 (hardcover) — ISBN 978-1-4263-7813-3 (lib. bdg.)

Manufactured in the United States of America
10 9 8 7 6 5 4 3 2 1

The authorized representative in the EU for product safety and compliance is Penguin Random House Ireland, Morrison Chambers, 32 Nassau Street, Dublin D02 YH68, Ireland, https://eu-contact.penguin.ie.

WANNA BE A
GREEK MYTHOLOGY
KNOW-IT-ALL?

Since you've read _Greeking Out_, you're well on your way. But there's more to discover! This Weird But True! book, full of fun facts, maps, and stories, is a handy guide to who's who and what's what in the amazing and a-MUSE-ing mythological world of the ancient Greeks.

AVAILABLE WHEREVER BOOKS ARE SOLD
Discover more at natgeokids.com

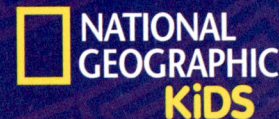